The Italians of America

This collection is a tribute to America's most significant Italians

By
Alfonso E. Panico

First published 1999 by Alfonso E. Panico
90 St. John Street
North Haven, Connecticut 06473

Library of Congress Catalog
Card Number is: 99-070053

ISBN: 0-9666075-5-4

Printed in the United States of America

Dedication

*To my family
and
The Italians of America*

ALFONSO E. PANICO

Alfonso E. Panico has previously published *The Italians of the New New Haven.* He has been very active in the Italian and Italian-American community for many years promoting Italian heritage and culture. He is on the board of directors of the Italian American Historical Society of New Haven, Connecticut, and a member of the National Italian American Foundation. Mr. Panico is past President, past General Chairman, and past Chairman of the Board of the Columbus Day Committee Inc. of New Haven. From 1990 to 1996, he served as Representative of the *Committee of Italians Abroad,* New York and Connecticut, established by the Italian government with its headquarters in New York. Mr. Panico, since 1974, has been the Connecticut correspondent of the national daily Italian newspaper *Il Progresso* and *America Oggi.*

CONTENTS

PREFACE

There are few experiences that temper the human condition comparable to leaving your place of birth, traveling across an ocean amidst the sounds and smells of steerage and arriving in a new land, without knowing its language or its customs, being only vaguely aware of its full opportunities and learning, quickly enough, that discrimination and prejudice is directed against all that is in you that is valuable. It was not an experience unique to Italians who sought to make America their home. But it was an experience that needs to be understood in order to appreciate the reasons for the accomplishments of those individuals of Italian-American heritage that Alfonso Panico has selected for this collection. They are, in his experience and judgement, men and women who, in a generation, have attained a form of recognition acclaimed widely in this new land, while holding tight to the values that once were ridiculed.

Alfonso Panico has undertaken a useful task. He is well-equipped to perform it. His service activities within the New Haven community have been consistent and consequential. He writes regularly about the life of New Haven through the Italian language newspaper, *Il Progresso*, for which he wrote for 20 years, and now for *America Oggi*, often using his skills to encourage and promote those who exemplified important community service. He demonstrated special leadership when, in 1985, he proposed and generated considerable support for renaming Wooster Square — in the heart of New Haven's historic Italian-American community — to Columbus Square; and has served yearly as an active and knowledgeable member of the Columbus Day Committee and the Italian Historical Society of New Haven. His participation has helped assure both institutions are highly regarded and successful.

Mr. Panico has continued, as well, to be active through The Committee of Italians Abroad, in New York and Connecticut, and through his position as the Italian Consulate Representative. In both of these positions he has provided thoughtful, humane guidance and support. He brought all these experiences to bear on the choices he has made here.

Missing from this collection, of course, are the parents and grandparents who endured the harshness of America, so that their children — those in this collection — could endure and prosper. For those who witnessed or felt the consequence of the lynching of Italian immigrants and the invasions and destruction of their neighborhoods, or who supported with dollars and time the defense of Sacco and Vanzetti or watched as neighbors or family were interned during WWII, no form of gratitude or praise could suffice. Missing as well are the millions of other Italian-Americans throughout the Nation, who daily raise families and work hard to assure the values they hold dear will be passed on to their children and reflected in their lives. Their successes may be measured differently but, in their own way, they are no less easily attained or worthy of commemoration by each of us.

In the end, the truest measure of "leadership" is not to forget the essential, distinguishing values of being Italian-American and to assure that the harshness that greeted our ancestors no longer forms a part of what otherwise must make America a place of welcome and opportunity for all people.

Neil Thomas Proto

Neil Thomas Proto
New Haven, Connecticut and Washington, D.C.
June, 1999

Mr. Proto is an Attorney and Adjunct Professor of Public Policy at Georgetown University.

RUDOLPH W. GIULIANI
Mayor - City of New York

Mayor Rudolph William Giuliani was born in Brooklyn, New York, on May 28, 1944, the only child of Helen Davanzo and Harold Giuliani. As a grandson of Italian immigrants from Naples and Tuscany, Rudy Giuliani learned a strong work ethic and a deep respect for America's ideal of equal opportunity.

Before his election in 1993 as the107th Mayor of the City of New York, Giuliani served as U.S. Attorney for the Southern District of New York, where he spearheaded the effort to jail drug dealers, fight organized crime, break the web of corruption in government, and prosecute white-collar criminals. Few U.S. Attorneys in history can match his record of 4,152 convictions with only 25 reversals.

Mayor Giuliani was re-elected to a second term in 1997 (the last time New York returned a Republican Mayor to office was 1941). As only the third Italian-American Mayor of New York City, Giuliani emulated one of his personal heroes, reform-minded Fiorello LaGuardia, by challenging the status quo and not shying away from controversy. Mayor Giuliani has returned accountability to city government. Once notorious around the world for its dangerous streets, New York is now recognized by the F.B.I. as the safest large city in America. Not only are the public assistance rolls no longer escalating, but they have decreased. New York City's workfare program is the largest and most successful in the country. Mayor Giuliani cut taxes and organized crime's stranglehold on various city businesses and industries, helping New York City's economy surge. As news of the city's renaissance spread worldwide, tourism has soared to record levels. To turn around the nation's largest urban public education system, Mayor Giuliani has worked tirelessly to restore accountability and raise standards throughout the city's schools.

FRANCO MODIGLIANI
Nobel Prize Recipient in Economic Science

Dr. Franco Modigliani was born on June 18, 1918 in Rome, the son of Dr. Enrico Modigliani and Dr. Olga Slascel. He received the Doctor of Jurisprudence degree from the University of Rome in 1939; the Doctor of Social Science degree from the New School for Social Research in 1944; an LLD degree (ad Honorem), University of Chicago, in 1967; a Doctor in Economics (Honoris Causa) from the University Catholique de Louvain in 1974; a Doctor Honoris of Humane Letters from Bard College, New York, in 1985; a Doctor of Humane Letters from Brandels University in 1986; and an Honorary Doctorate degree from the University of Hartford in 1988. He was a Fulbright Lecturer at the University of Rome and Palermo, Italy. Dr. Modigliani became an American citizen in 1946. Currently, he is Institute Professor Emeritus at the Alfred P. Sloan School of Management of the Massachusetts Institute of Technology, and has been a contributor to many different areas of economics and finance, such as monetary theory, capital markets, corporation finance, public finance, international economics and macroeconomics. In 1970, Dr. Modigliani was appointed Institute Professor, an appointment that MIT reserves for scholars of special distinction to recognize accomplishments of leadership of high intellectual quality. In 1985, Dr. Modigliani was the recipient of the *Alfred Nobel Memorial Prize in Economic Science,* and he received also the James R. Killian Faculty Achievement Award from MIT. The Franco Modigliani Professorship of financial economics at MIT, an endowed chair, was established in 1995 to permanently recognize Dr. Modigliani's multiple contributions to the field. Dr. Modigliani is the author of 18 books, five volumes of his collected works, and numerous articles for economic journals.

ANTONIN SCALIA
Justice - United States Supreme Court

Justice Antonin Scalia was born on March 11,1936 in Trenton, New Jersey. He attended Georgetown University and the University of Fribourg (Switzerland) earning an A.B. In 1960 he received his L.L.B. from Harvard where he was also a note editor of the *Harvard Law Review*, and a Sheldon Fellow.

In 1962, Justice Scalia was admitted to the Ohio Bar, and in 1970 to the Virginia Bar. He started his private practice with Jones, Day, Cockley and Reavis in Cleveland, Ohio.

On August 17, 1982, he was nominated by President Ronald Reagan to the U.S. Court of Appeals for the District of Columbia. Four years later in 1986, President Reagan appointed him Associate Justice of the United States Supreme Court, becoming the first Italian-American member of the Supreme Court.

Considered by many an outspoken conservative and a possible presidential candidate, Justice Scalia has often criticized Supreme Court decisions on abortions and affirmative action. Since his appointment to the United States Supreme Court, he has fought tirelessly for a Constitution of real meaning and for a democracy under the rule of law rather than the rule of men.

Justice Scalia has written many articles, among which is an important essay *A Matter of Interpretation: Federal Courts and the Law.* He has been editor of the *Regulation Magazine*, chairman of the ABA Conference of Section, and has been on the board of visitors, J. Reuben Clark Law School, and Brigham Young University During President Nixon's administration, he served as general counsel for the White House Office of Telecommunication Policy. He was married to Maureen McCarthy on September 10, 1960, and has nine children.

BARONESS MARIUCCIA ZERILLI-MARIMO'
Founder and Chairman - Casa Italiana Zerilli-Marimo'- NYU

Baroness Mariuccia Zerilli-Marimo' was born in Milano, Italy. She graduated from the University of Lausanne, Switzerland, and served for many years as
the National Secretary of the Italian League of Women Voters. An accomplished
scholar and polyglot (she is fluent in Italian, French, Spanish, English and Portu-
guese), throughout her marriage, she participated in numerous cultural, business
and diplomatic activities along with her husband, Baron Guido Zerilli-Marimo', a
distinguished industrialist who also served as Ambassador to Ethiopia and Portugal.
After her husband's death, the Baroness, in continuity with his legacy, has undertaken an intense philanthropic activity in Europe as well as in the United States. In
memory of her husband, she donated to New York University, where she is a Trustee,
the Winfield Scott House, which, built in 1851, was designated a National Historic
Landmark in 1974. After personally overseeing its extensive renovations and refur-
bishing, she has turned the distinguished residence, with its 13,800 square-foot interior, 88 seat auditorium, seminar and conference room, into one of the most recognized centers of cultural, economic, scientific and educational exchange between
Italy and the United States. Her unrelenting work continues also for the promotion
of Italian heritage by establishing annual awards; the most recent of which, the
Premio Zerilli-Marimo' for Italian Fiction, the first of its kind. The Baroness is
Chairman of the Board of the Casa Italiana Center of Italian Studies, and is Chairman of La Scala Foundation USA and her newly created FOSTER (Foundation for
Science and Technology Education and Research) which brings together the best of
Italian and American research scientists. The Baroness is currently serving as a Del-
egate of the Holy See Mission to the United Nations.

GUIDO CALABRESI
United States Circuit Judge for the Second District

Judge Guido Calabresi is one of the most prominent figures in New Haven, Connecticut, well known and respected in the U.S. and abroad. He was appointed United States Circuit Judge in July, 1994. Prior to his appointment, Judge Calabresi was Dean and Sterling Professor at the Yale Law School from 1985 to 1994. He continues to serve as a member of the faculty at the Yale Law School, where he began teaching in 1959 at the age of 29. He is presently Sterling Professor of Law Emeritus and Professorial Lecturer.

Judge Calabresi, the author of numerous articles and books, is known worldwide for his path-breaking work on tort law. His first article, *Some Thoughts on Risk Distribution and the Law of Torts* (1961), helped launch the modern law of economics movement. His now classic book, *The Costs of Accidents* (1970) is widely recognized as the first general theory of civil liability since Oliver Wendell Holmes's *The Common Law* (1889) and was the basis of many reforms in the law of torts in the past 20 years.

Born in Milano, Italy, October 18, 1932, Judge Calabresi emigrated to this country with his family in 1939 for political reasons. He became a naturalized citizen upon his parents' naturalization in 1948. His father, Massimo Calabresi, was a cardiologist and professor at the Yale School of Medicine. His mother, Bianca Finzi Contini Calabresi, a scholar of comparative literature, was professor and chairman of Italian at Albertus Magnus College in New Haven. He is married to Anne Tyler Calabresi and has three children.

Judge Calabresi holds a B.S., summa cum laude from Yale College, 1953, a B.A. degree with First Class Honors from Oxford University, in 1955, an LLB degree, magna cum laude, in 1958 from Yale Law School, and an M.A. in Politics, Philosophy and Economics from Oxford University in 1959. A Rhodes Scholar, he has been awarded 20 honorary degrees from universities in the United States, Canada, Italy and Sweden. In 1958-59, he served as clerk to U.S. Supreme Court Justice Hugo Black. He also served as the note Editor of the *Yale Law Journal*, 1957-58, while graduating first in his law school class.

ANTHONY CARDINAL BEVILACQUA
Cardinal of Philadelphia

Cardinal Anthony Joseph Bevilacqua was born in Brooklyn, New York on June 17, 1923. He was one of 11 children born to Luigi and Maria Bevilacqua. Following his 1943 graduation from Cathedral College, he attended Immaculate Conception Seminary in Huntington, New York. There he completed the six years of philosophy and theology requirements and was ordained on June 11, 1949 at St. James Cathedral, Brooklyn. In 1956, he received his Doctorate in Canon Law (J.C.D.) *Summa Cum Laude* from Rome's Gregorian University. He attended Columbia University where he received his Masters in Political Science (M.A.) in 1962. Ten years later he began his studies in Civil Law and in 1975 he received a degree in Civil Law (J.D.) from St. John's University Law School in Queens, New York. In 1971, he established Brooklyn's Catholic Migration and Refugee Office, and on November 24, 1980, he was ordained a Bishop. He served as Auxiliary Bishop and Chancellor of the Brooklyn Diocese. On December 8, 1987, Pope John Paul II appointed him Archbishop of Philadelphia. His installation took place on February 11, 1988. Three years later, on May 29, 1991, Pope John Paul II announced that Archbishop Bevilacqua's elevation to the College of Cardinals would take place in a consistory on June 28,1991. During his tenure in Philadelphia, Cardinal Bevilacqua has made spiritual renewal of the faithful a priority and has undertaken an active pastoral ministry.

Cardinal Bevilacqua is currently a member of the Pontifical Council *Cor Unum,* and a member of many congregations and committees. He is admitted to practice as a civil lawyer before the Courts of New York State, the Courts of the State of Pennsylvania and the U.S. Supreme Court.

LEE IACOCCA
Former CEO and Chairman of Chrysler Corporation

Lee A. Iacocca was born on October 15, 1924 in Allentown, Pennsylvania. He earned a Bachelor of Science degree in industrial engineering from Lehigh University in Pennsylvania, and a master's degree in mechanical engineering from Princeton University.

Mr. Iacocca joined Chrysler in November of 1978 and retired in December of 1992. Before Chrysler, he was with Ford Motor Company for 32 years. During his career at Ford, he rose from Management Trainee to President and Chief Operating Officer and a member of Ford's Board of Directors, serving in those capacities until October 1978. Mr. Iacocca always dreamed of putting together a car company called Global Motors to design, market and distribute electric vehicles and unite the best of the U.S., Europe and Asia. In 1997, he finally founded the EV Global Motors Company, to move the electric vehicle industry from theory to reality. Today, he is Chairman and CEO of EV Global Motors.

Mr. Iacocca is the author of two best-selling books, *Iacocca* and *Talking Straight*, and from 1985 to 1992, wrote a nationally syndicated newspaper column. He has received honorary doctorate degrees from many distinguished colleges and universities. He is also Chairman Emeritus of Statue of Liberty-Ellis Island Foundation, and is a member of the Advisory Board of the nation's largest reading motivation program, Reading is Fundamental, a non-profit organization founded in 1968. In addition, Mr. Iacocca is an Honorary Trustee of Lehigh University. In 1987, he was named Founder and Chairman of the Advisory Board of Iacocca Institute at Lehigh University. He is also chairman of the Committee for Corporate Support of the Joslin Diabetes Foundation.

GEORGE E. PATAKI
Governor - New York State

Governor George E. Pataki was born on June 24,1945, in Peekskill, Westchester County, the son of Margaret Lagana Pataki and Louie Pataki. He graduated from Peekskill High School. In 1967, he graduated from Yale and in 1970 graduated from Columbia Law School, both of which he attended on academic scholarships. In 1981, he was elected the youngest mayor ever of the City of Peekskill, and was re-elected in 1983 with 76% of the vote, the largest plurality in the city's history. In 1984, Governor Pataki was elected to the State Assembly, representing the Mid-Hudson River region. As an Assemblyman, he was named "State Legislator of the Year" by the Environmental Planning Lobby, a coalition of more than 100 New York environmental groups. During his terms in Assembly, Governor Pataki co-sponsored the Hudson River Estuary Management Act, Solid Waste Management Act of 1988 and Hudson Valley Greenway Council and numerous other important environmental initiatives.

Governor Pataki was elected to the New York Senate in 1992, serving the 37th district in the Mid-Hudson region. He also served as chairman in the Senate Ethics Committee and was named the "Environmental Champion of the Year" by the League of Conservation Voters Education Fund. In 1994, Governor Pataki was elected the 53rd Governor of New York State, becoming New York State's first Republican-Conservative chief executive. His mandate was to bring sweeping and fundamental change to a state that had suffered under years of failed policies. During his tenure, in the tradition of his hero, Theodore Roosevelt, Governor Pataki has taken bold steps toward protecting New York State's precious natural resources for generations to come, while continuing to promote economic growth.

1996 - The Mayor of New York City, Rudolph Giuliani, entertains
Oscar Luigi Scalfaro, President of Italy.

New York - March 1999 - On the occasion of the presentation of the Award of Excellence
by Governor Pataki to soprano Licia Albanese. From left are: Margareth Lagana' Pataki,
mother of Governor Pataki; Consul General of Italy Giorgio Radicati, Licia Albanese,
renowned soprano at the Metropolitan Opera of New York, Claudia Massimo Berns,
assistant to Governor Pataki for Italian Affairs.

HUGO V. RIZZOLI
Chairman - Department of Neurological Surgery GWU

Dr. Hugo Victor Rizzoli was born in Newark, New Jersey, the son of Angelo and Clelia Rizzoli. His parents immigrated to America from Calabritto, a town near Salerno, Italy. He received his A. B. degree from Johns Hopkins University in 1936, and his M.D. degree from Johns Hopkins University in 1940. He interned in Medicine and later entered the Surgery program at Johns Hopkins Hospital. In 1942, he became a Harvey Cushing Fellow, and he served as a Neurological Resident on Dr. Walter Dandy's service. Upon completion of his residency in October 1944, he entered the United States Medical Corps and served as a Neurosurgeon, first at Halloran General Hospital on Staten Island, and in 1945, he was transferred to Walter Reed General Hospital. During his last year at Walter Reed he was Chief of the Neurosurgical Section. Dr. Rizzoli was discharged in November 1946, with the rank of Major. He immediately entered the private practice of Neurological Surgery and became Chief of Neurosurgery at Emergency Hospital and joined the Faculty and Voluntary Staff of Neurological Surgery at the George Washington University Hospital. In 1958, Emergency Hospital and two other hospital amalgamated and built the Washington Hospital Center, where he was the first Chief of the Department of Neurological Surgery, and a member of the Board of Trustees. In 1969, he became the first full time Professor and Chairman of the Department of Neurological Surgery at George Washington University Medical Center, serving until 1987, and was then appointed Professor Emeritus in Residence. Dr. Rizzoli co-authored three books on post operative complications in neurosurgical practice. He was listed among the Finest Specialists in the book *Best Doctors in the U.S.* On October 17,1998, The Hugo V. Rizzoli Chair of Neurological Surgery was established at George Washington University.

LEONARD RIGGIO
Chairman and CEO - Barnes & Noble, Inc.

Leonard Riggio was born in New York City. He is the founder, chairman and chief executive officer of Barnes & Noble, Inc., the parent company of Barnes & Noble Bookstores, B. Dalton Booksellers, and Doubleday Book Shops. He is also the chairman and major shareholder of several privately held companies including Barnes & Noble College Bookstores, the largest operator of college bookstores in the country, serving more than 300 universities and colleges across America. Mr. Riggio began his career as a bookseller in 1958, when he went to work at New York University Bookstore while attending college at night. In 1965, he opened his first bookstore, called SBX, in Greenwich Village, serving local college students. In 1971, Mr. Riggio acquired the trade name Barnes & Noble and its single store, adding it to his already existing group of stores. After successfully bringing Barnes & Noble into the trade book business, he created the nation's first group of discount stores. In 1986, Mr. Riggio acquired B. Dalton Booksellers. The company continues to grow at an accelerated pace through innovative retail strategies and acquisitions. Barnes & Noble stores stock an authoritative selection of more than 175,000 titles and more than 27,000 publishers with an emphasis on small, independent publishers and university presses. The company is the world's largest bookseller on the World Wide Web (http://www.barnesandnoble.com), and the exclusive bookseller on America Online's Marketplace (keyword: B*arnesandNoble*). Mr. Riggio is chairman of the board of Dia Center for the Arts and many other organizations. He has received the Ellis Island Medal of Honor, Frederick Douglas Medallion and an honorary doctor's degree from Baruch College of the City University of New York.

L. JAY OLIVA
President - New York University

Dr. L.J. Oliva was born in 1933 in Walden, New York. He has a B.A. from Manhattan College, and an M.A. and Ph.D. from Syracuse University. He was a University Fellow at Syracuse, a Fribourg Fellow at the University of Paris, and a member of Phi Beta Kappa.

Dr. L. Jay Oliva began teaching Russian history at NYU over 35 years ago, later becoming Dean of University College. In 1983, he became Chancellor and Executive Vice-President for Academic Affairs. On November 21, 1991, Dr. Oliva was inaugurated as the 14th president of New York University, the first faculty member in the 165-year history of the institution to be elevated to this position.

His vision has proved crucial to the long-term growth and development of the university community. This vision has helped energize the administration's successful efforts to built a campus of the city, including a major growth in the international studies, and support for research work of the faculty while maintaining a high level of classroom instruction.

Dr. Oliva is the author and editor of numerous works on Russian and European history. His fields of academic specialization are 18th century Russia, Russian diplomatic history and 18th century Europe. Dr. Oliva has received a number of awards and honorary degrees among which is a Doctorate of Philosophy honorary degree from Tel Aviv University, a Doctorate of Law honorary degree from Saint Thomas Aquinas College, a Doctorate of Literature honorary degree from University College Dublin, a Doctorate of Humane Letters honorary degree from the Manhattan College. Dr. Oliva was decorated a *chevalier* of the French Legion of Honor.

A. BARTLETT GIAMATTI
Yale University President - Commissioner of Baseball

Dr. Angelo Bartlett Giamatti was born in Boston, Massachusetts, on April 4, 1938. His father, Valentine, was a Yale graduate and Professor Emeritus of Italian at Mount Holyoke College. His mother, Mary Claybaugh Walton, was a graduate of Smith College. After graduating from Phillips Academy in Andover, MA, he entered Yale, where he majored in English. In 1960, he received a Bachelors' degree, magna cum laude and went to graduate school as a Woodrow Wilson Fellow, obtaining a doctorate in comparative literature in 1964.

Dr. Giamatti, a scholar in the field of Renaissance literature, joined the Yale faculty in 1966 as an assistant professor of English, became an associate professor of English and comparative literature in 1970, and full professor in 1971. Before joining the Yale faculty, he taught Italian and comparative literature at Princeton University.

In December 1977, at the age of 40, Dr. Giamatti was named the 19th president of Yale University. Under his leadership, the size of endowment and alumni contributions rose substantially. He presided over Yale when more than 2,600 clerical and technical workers, members of Local 34 and 35 of the Federation of University Employees, went on strike.

Dr. Giamatti was a remarkable and talented man with a great sense of humor. He loved New Haven, Yale and had a passion for sports, with particular interest in baseball. In 1985, announced his resignation as Yale president effective June 1986, when he was named National League president. In 1989, he became baseball commissioner. Dr. Giamatti was a recipient of numerous honorary degrees and was the author of many articles and books. He died on September 1, 1989, at the age of 51, after suffering a heart attack at his summer home on Martha's Vineyard.

"KING BART"

New Haven, April 24, 1982 - Human Chess Board Game at
Yale University Campus - Yale President Bart Giamatti.

"KING BEN"

New Haven, April 24, 1982 - Human Chess Board Game at
Yale University Campus - Mayor Biagio Di Lieto.

NEIL THOMAS PROTO
Professor - Attorney at Law

Neil Thomas Proto is an environmental lawyer and partner in the Washington, D.C. law firm of Verner, Liipfert, Bernhard, McPherson and Hand and an Adjunct Professor of Public Policy at Georgetown University. He was born and raised in New Haven, Connecticut, and attended its public schools. He received his Bachelor of Arts from Southern Connecticut State University (1987), and Master of Arts in International Affairs (1969) and his Juris Doctor (1972) from the George Washington University. His mother, Celeste, was born in Ripacandida (Basilicata) and immigrated to New Haven in 1916, at age 6. His father, Matthew, served for two decades as New Haven's Assistant Registrar of Voters.

From 1972 to 1979, Mr. Proto served as an environmental attorney with the Environment and Natural Resources Division of the United States Department of Justice, where he argued cases before the nation's United States Courts of Appeals involving natural resources, environmental and Native American issues. He was awarded the Department Special Commendation Award for Outstanding Service. In 1980 and 1981, Mr. Proto also served as general counsel to President Carter's Nuclear Safety Oversight Committee, chaired by then Arizona Governor Bruce Babbitt.

Within New Haven, Mr. Proto twice chaired the inaugurations of Mayor Biagio Di Lieto in 1980 and 1982,which were the first ever held on the Yale University Campus.

Mr. Proto has written and spoken on various legal and environmental issues, as well as the history, legal matters, art, poetry and cultural impacts of the controversy over the lives of Bartolomeo Vanzetti and Nicola Sacco.

1999 - Mayor of New York, Rudolph Giuliani, gives the State of the City address.

1999 - From left are Mena Ricciardi, the Consul General of Italy, Giorgio Radicati and Cristiana Pegoraro, famous Italian pianist, during a concert at Carnegie Hall, New York.

FRANK C. CARLUCCI
U.S. Secretary of Defense

Frank C. Carlucci was born on October 18, 1930. His grandfather Frank Carlucci was born in Santomenna, Salerno, Italy. He is currently chairman and partner in the Carlyle Group, a Washington, D.C.-based merchant bank.

Prior to joining the Carlyle Group in 1989, Mr. Carlucci served as Secretary of Defense from 1987 to 1989. Previously, in 1987, he served as President Reagan's National Security Advisor.

From 1983 to 1987, before returning to government service, Mr. Carlucci was Chairman and CEO of Sears World Trade. His government service included positions such as Deputy Secretary of Defense (1980-82), Deputy Director of Central Intelligence (1978-80), Ambassador to Portugal (1975-78), Under Secretary of Health Education and Welfare (1973-75), Deputy Director of Office of Economic Opportunity (1970-72), and Director of the Office of Economic Opportunity (1969). Mr. Carlucci was a Foreign Service Officer from 1956 to 1980.

Mr. Carlucci serves on the following corporate boards: Ashland Inc.; Kaman Corporation; Neurogen Corporation; Northern Telecom Limited; The Quaker Oats Company; SunResorts, Ltd., N.V.; Texas Biotechnology Corporation; Pharmacia 7 Upjohn, Inc.; the Directors Advisory Council of New York City Division of Manufacturers and Traders Trust Company, and Board of Trustees for the RAND Corporation. Among the numerous awards and honors are: The National Intelligence Distinguished Service Medal, Herbert Roback Memorial Award, George C. Marshall Award, Woodrow Wilson Award, James Forrestal Award, the Presidential Citizens Award, and the Defense Department Distinguished Civilian Service Award. He also received an Honorary Doctor of Law degree from the University of Scranton.

1985 : On behalf of His Holiness John Paul II, John Cardinal O'Connor, Archbishop of New York, confers the Pontifical Knighthood (in rank of Grand Cross of the Order of St. Gregory the Great) upon New York State Supreme Court Justice Dominic Massaro.

1996 - President of Italy, Oscar Luigi Scalfaro (left), and Ambassador Francesco Paolo Fulci (right), welcome the Italian community during a reception at the United Nations in New York.

FRANCIS FORD COPPOLA
Producer - Director - Writer

Francis Ford Coppola, the son of composer and musician Carmine Coppola, was born on April 7, 1939, and grew up in Queens and Long Island, New York, where his family settled shortly after his birth. As a young boy, he turned out 8mm features edited from home movies. At the age of nine, he was left almost paralyzed by polio. Bedridden and isolated for almost a year, he developed an interest in comic books, puppetry, ventriloquism and television.

Mr. Coppola's early interest in the arts led to a major in theater at New York's Hofstra University and a M.F.A. in film from UCLA. He entered Hofstra in 1955 to major in theater arts and became a driving force in the drama department, breaking new grounds in student production; and was the founder of still extant: SPECRUM PLAYERS. However, when Mr. Coppola viewed Eisenstein's *Ten Days That Shook The World,* cinema became his passion. While at Hofstra, he founded the cinema workshop, contributed to the campus literary magazine and won three H.D. Lawrence Awards for theatrical production and direction, and received the Beckerman Award for his outstanding contributions to the theater arts division of the school. After earning his B.A. in theater arts in 1959, he enrolled at UCLA for graduate work in films, and supported himself by occasionally working as an editor on the new fad of the day: nudie films. While still at UCLA, Mr. Coppola worked as an all-purpose assistant to Roger Corman on a variety of modestly budgeted but lucrative films. He became later very popular and very well respected for his work in the U.S. and abroad. Among his acclaimed movies, *Apocalypse Now, One from The Heart, The Godfather Part III, The Outsiders,* and John Grisham's *The Rainmaker.*

GERALDINE A. FERRARO
United States Representative

United States Representative Geraldine A. Ferraro, was born in Newburgh, New York, the daughter of Antonetta Corierri and Dominic Ferraro. Before entering politics, Congresswoman Ferraro taught elementary school in New York City Public Schools for five years. During that time, she also attended Fordham Law School at night. After spending 13 years at home raising her three children, she joined the Queens County District Attorney's Office. She started the Special Victims Bureau, supervising the prosecution of sex crimes, child abuse, domestic violence and violent crimes against senior citizens. In 1978, Congresswoman Ferraro was first elected to Congress from New York's 9th Congressional District in Queens. Her Committee assignments in Congress included the Public Works Committee, Post Office and Civil Service Committee, the Budget Committee, and the Select Committee on Aging, where she was an advocate for the elderly, fighting proposed cuts in Social Security and Medicare. Congresswoman Ferraro earned a place in history as the first woman vice-presidential candidate on a national party ticket. From 1996 to 1998, she was a co-host of *Crossfire*, a political interview program on CNN. In 1994, she was appointed the United States Ambassador to the United Nations Human Rights Commission by President Clinton and served in that position through 1996. Congresswoman Ferraro has written many articles and three books, *My Story, Geraldine Ferraro; Changing History,* and *Framing a Life.* She has honorary degrees from a number of colleges and universities nationwide, and she currently serves as a board member of the Fordham Law School Board of Visitors, the New York Easter Seal Society, the National Italian Foundation, and the Board of Advocates of the Planned Parenthood Federation of America,

1989 - Liberty State Park, N.J. - Congressman Peter Rodino
of N.J., welcomes the President of Italy, Francesco Cossiga.

June 12, 1971 - Philadelphia - United States Conference of Mayors. Seated, left to right, Mayor John
V. Lindsay, New York City; Mayor Joseph L. Alioto, San Francisco; Mayor Frank Zullo, Norwalk,
Connecticut. Mr. Zullo was elected Mayor of Norwalk in 1965, at age 33. He served for three terms.

MARIO ANDRETTI
The Greatest Race Driver of all time

Mario Andretti was born in Montona, Italy, the son of Rina and Alvise Luigi Andretti. He and his twin brother, Aldo, were born during the beginning of World War II. When the war ended, the peninsula of Istria, which is near the town of Montona, became part of Yugoslavia, and they were trapped inside a Communist country. For seven years, from 1948 to 1955, the family lived in a refugee camp. They waited a long time for U.S. visas. When the visas were finally granted, the Andretti left all their belongings behind and began their new life in the United States. Settling in Nazareth, Pennsylvania in June 1955, the family of five had only $125 and didn't speak English. A few days after arriving in America, the Andretti boys were working at an uncle's garage when a station wagon pulled in towing a sprint car. It wasn't long before they figured out that there was a race track nearby. Suddenly they had a whole new passion for life, and with some local friends they built a sports car and raced it for the first time in March of 1959. His brother Aldo retired from racing in 1969 after a major accident. Meanwhile, Mr. Andretti's career flourished as he won 20 races in his first two seasons. Thereafter, he won just about everything: The Indy 500, The Daytona 500, The Indy Car Championship four times. He has been World Formula One Champion. He has won in sports cars, sprint cars and stock cars. Mr. Andretti was named Driver of the Quarter of Century, and he is enshrined in the Indianapolis 500 Hall of Fame, the Sprint Car Hall of Fame and the Motor Sports Hall of Fame. Mr. Andretti's name has become a symbol of excellence, dedication, pride and victory. He retired from active driving at the end of 1994, and he is now a successful businessman and serves as spokesman, associate and friend to top executives around the world.

JACK VALENTI
Chairman and CEO of the Motion Picture Association

Jack Valenti was born in Houston, Texas. He began work as a 16 year old office boy with the Humble Oil Company (now Exxon). As a young pilot in the Army Corps in World War II, Lieutenant Valenti flew 51 combat missions as the pilot-commander of a B-25 attack bomber with the 12th Air Force in Italy. He was decorated with the Distinguished Flying Cross, the Air Medal with four clusters, the Distinguished Unit Citation with one cluster, and the European Theatre Ribbon with four battle stars. Mr. Valenti earned a B.A. from the University of Houston doing all his undergraduate work at night and working during the day. He graduated with a M.B.A. from Harvard. In 1952, he co-founded the advertising/political counseling agency of Weekley & Valenti. In 1955, he met the man who would have the largest impact on his life, the then Majority Leader of the U.S. Senate, Lyndon B. Johnson. Mr. Valenti's agency was in charge of the press during the visit of President Kennedy and Vice President Johnson to Texas. Mr. Valenti was in the motorcade in Dallas on November 22, 1963, and within an hour of the murder of John F. Kennedy, Mr. Valenti was on Air Force One flying back to Washington, the first newly hired Special Assistant to the President. On June 1,1966, Mr. Valenti resigned his White House post to become the leader of the Motion Picture Association, only the third man in MPA history to become its leader.

Mr. Valenti has written four books and numerous essays for the *New York Times, The Washington Post, Los Angeles Times, Reader's Digest, Newsweek* and many other publications. France conferred him its highly prized Legion d'Honneur, the French Legion of honor. He has been awarded his own Star on the Hollywood Walk of Fame.

DOMINIC R. MASSARO
Justice - Supreme Court of New York

Named to the state judiciary by Governor Cuomo in 1984, Justice Massaro is a legal author and lecturer on both sides of the Atlantic. He holds advanced degrees in economics, government, criminal justice and jurisprudence, and served both as New York City and state human rights commissioner. President Nixon named him to the Appeals Board of the Selective Service System. He was United States regional Director of Action (Peace Corps, Vista, Older American Programs), with jurisdiction from New York to the Caribbean, during the Ford Administration.

Justice Massaro is a Knight of the Grand Cross of the Italian Republic, Italy's highest civilian designation. He is president emeritus of the Conference of Presidents of Major Italian American Organizations. In 1983, he received the Congressional Medal of Merit. John Paul II accorded him the highest dignity for a Catholic layman: Pontifical Knight. For 20 years , he served as chairman of Cardinal's Committee on Italian Apostolate of the Archdiocese of New York. He was named "Catholic New Yorker." In 1991, his volume *Cesare Beccaria - The Father of Criminal Justice: His Impact on Anglo American Jurisprudence* (Int'l. U. Press) earned him the International Dorso Prize. In 1994, he was the joint recipient of the "Lehman-La Guardia Award in Civil Rights" by the Order Sons of Italy in America and Anti Defamation League of B'nai B'rith. Unico National gave him its " Rizzuto Award," highest in 1985. A long time director of the National Italian American Foundation, Justice Massaro is a past president of the National Commission for Social Justice and of the Gramercy Boys Club of New York. The jurist is a Woodrow Wilson Fellow, and is completing his sixth year as the representative of the American Judges Association to the United Nations.

ROBERT C. ZAMPANO
United States District Court Judge

Retired U.S. District Judge Robert C. Zampano has had an extraordinary legal career.

After his graduation from Yale Law School in 1954, Judge Zampano clerked with U.S. District Judge Robert P. Anderson in New Haven, Connecticut. In private practice, Judge Zampano tried scores of cases in the state and federal courts, specializing in the trial of Federal Employer's Liability Act cases. He never lost a jury trial and received some of the highest verdicts of the era.

After six years in private practice, the federal judges appointed Judge Zampano Acting U.S. Attorney of the District of Connecticut and President John F. Kennedy later appointed him to a full term. After nine years of practice, President Lyndon B. Johnson appointed him a U.S. District Judge, a position he held for 30 years. He was one of the youngest lawyers ever to serve in both positions. From 1989 to 1994, he was also a Clinical Professor (adjunct) of Law at Yale Law School.

Since his retirement from the federal bench in 1994, Judge Zampano has devoted his efforts to the resolution of cases as a full-time arbitrator and mediator with Mediation Consultants, LLC. He has become one of the most well-respected mediators in the country, earning a national reputation for his extraordinary efforts in settling a wide variety of complex disputes.

Judge Zampano is the recipient of many awards, has published numerous articles on settlement and is the author of *Courtroom Success: A View From The Bench.*

JOSEPH LA PALOMBARA
Chairman - Political Science Department - Yale University

Dr. Joseph La Palombara is the Arnold Wolfers Professor of Political Science and Management at Yale University. A native of Chicago, he is a graduate of the University of Illinois (A.B., MA.) and Princeton University (M.A., Ph.D.). He has been at Yale since 1964. He has taught at Oregon State, Princeton and Michigan Stateuniversities, and has held visiting professorships at Columbia University, the University of California (Berkeley) and the University of Florence.

Dr. La Palombara has chaired the Departments of Political Science at Michigan State and Yale. He has also been the director (1987-1992) of Yale's Institution for Social and Policy Studies. He currently chairs the International Academic Committee of the Tel Aviv International School of Management.

Dr. La Palombara is a member of the American Academy of Arts and Sciences, The Connecticut Academy of Arts and Sciences. He has held fellowships from the Center for Advanced Study in the Behavioral Sciences, the Social Science Research Council, and the Ford, Rockefeller and Guggenheim foundations. In the early 1980's, he served as First Secretary of the American Embassy at Rome, Italy.

The author of more than a dozen books and several hundred scientific papers and general interest articles, Dr. La Palombara is also editor-in-chief of the magazine, *Italy, Italy*. He was a founding partner and President of Multinational Strategies, Inc. (New York) and currently the President of the Italian-American Multimedia Corporation (New York). He has been a consultant to agencies of government, private foundations and many industries in the U.S. and Europe.

CARM COZZA
Yale's Head Football Coach

Carm Cozza was the Head Football Coach at Yale University for 32 years. During that time, he coached over 300 games with a total of 179 wins. His teams have won 10 Ivy League Championships, had 18 winning seasons, six Bushnell Cups, seven NCAA Post-Graduate Scholarship winners, seven First-Team CoSIDA Academic All-Americans, seven GTE/CoSIDA District I Academic All-Americans, five National Football Foundation Hall of Fame Scholar-Athletes and five Rhodes Scholars. During his tenure, he has had only six players fail to graduate.

Mr. Cozza graduated from Miami University of Ohio in 1952 (Master's Degree - 1959) where he won three letters apiece in football and baseball. While on the gridiron under the tutelage of Ara Parseghian and Woody Hayes, Mr. Cozza saw triple duty as a quarterback, running back and defensive back. In baseball, he pitched and played the outfield, posting a 1.50 earned run average and career batting average of .338. Mr. Cozza, who entered the Miami Hall of Fame in 1970, played baseball professionally in the Cleveland Indians and Chicago White Sox organizations.

Mr. Cozza has also coached in numerous all-star games. An assistant coach for the 1970 East-West Shine Game in Palo Alto, California, he served as a head coach in the 1972 contest. Mr. Cozza served as defensive coordinator in the 1981 Blue-Gray Classic in Mobile, Alabama. When the 1989 Ivy League All-Stars went to Tokyo for the first Epson Ivy Bowl, Mr. Cozza was the head coach of the Ancient Eight in it's victory over the Japanese College All-Stars.

JOE DiMAGGIO
Baseball Player - Hall of Fame

Joe DiMaggio was born on November 25, 1914 in Martinez, California. Recognized as baseball's "Greatest Player," Mr. DiMaggio ranks in the top five of every major offensive category in Yankees' history. Nicknamed "The Yankee Clipper," his lifetime .325 batting average is tied for third on the Yankees' all time list. He also ranks third in RBI and triples and fourth in runs, hits, doubles and home runs. Over a 13-year career from 1936 to 1951, Mr. DiMaggio was the leader of 10 pennant-winning and nine World-Championships.

Mr. DiMaggio was bought by the Yankees, and by the San Francisco Seals of the Pacific Coast League. As a member of the Seals, he hit in 61 consecutive games in 1933, the longest hitting streak in professional baseball history. He would play the 1935 season with the Seals before joining the Yankees in 1936 and was named MVP of the Pacific Coast League, batting .398 with 34 HR and 154 RBI.

After leading the Yankees to their second of four straight World Championship, in 1941, Mr. DiMaggio established a record hitting safely in a Major-League record 56 consecutive games. After the record streak was snapped, he hit safely in another 16 straight games. Mr. DiMaggio would bat .357 with 30 HR and 125 RBI that season, earning his second MVP Award and guiding the Yankees to their 5th World-Series Championship in six years.

After the 1951 season, Mr. DiMaggio retired, making the announcement on December 11, 1951. Upon his retirement, his uniform number "5" was retired by the Yankees and on April 12, 1970, the Yankees honored him by dedicating a plaque on the center-field wall of Yankee Stadium. He was named to the Hall of Fame in 1955. Mr. DiMaggio died March 8, 1999.

JOHN J. CALI
CEO Mack-Cali Real Estate Corp.

John J. Cali was born on August 8, 1918 in Bear Canyon, Colorado. His Sicilian parents, Vincenzo and Maria Grazia Drago, immigrated from Italy around the turn of the century. His father was a farmer in Sicily and soon became a miner in the lucrative anthracite mines of Bear Canyon. In 1929, when many mines were shut down, the entire family moved to New Jersey.

Mr. Cali attended Passaic and Clifton public schools. In 1937, he graduated from Clifton High School and entered Indiana University where, as a musician, he worked his way through school and received an A.B. degree in Psychology-Sociology. After World War II, Mr. Cali, and his brother Angelo and a business associate, invested with a home developer in a number of projects constructing single-family homes. Then, in early 1949, with his brother and a business associate, he decided to enter the development of single-family homes in New Jersey. In the late sixties, he decided to add suburban office development to his construction activities. Prior to taking his company public in 1994, Mr. Cali had spearheaded the development of over five million square feet of commercial properties. Since 1994, Mack-Cali Real Estate Corp., has grown to a company of over 27 million square feet of first class office and commercial properties, located in the Northeast, Southwest and Western United States.

Mr. Cali's rigid requirements for high-quality and aesthetically-appealing designs have won him and his company many awards for building excellence; among them "New Good Neighbor Awards" in the State of New Jersey. In 1990, his firm was named "Developer of the Year" by the National Association of Industrial and Office Parks.

LOUIS J. FREEH
Director - Federal Bureau of Investigation

Louis J. Freeh was born in Jersey City, New Jersey. His maternal grand-mother was born in Naples, and emigrated to the United States, where she gave birth to his mother. In 1974, he earned a J.D. degree from Rutgers Law School, and an LL.M. degree in criminal law from New York University Law School in 1984.

Director Freeh served as an FBI Special Agent from 1975 to 1981 in the New York City Field Office and at FBI Headquarters in Washington, D.C. In 1981, he joined the U.S. Attorney's Office. Subsequently, he held positions there as Chief of the Organized Crime Unit, Deputy U.S. Attorney, and Associate U.S. Attorney.

During this time, Director Freeh was the lead prosecutor in the "Pizza Con-nection" case, the largest and most complex investigation ever undertaken by the Federal Government. The case involved an extensive drug-trafficking operation in the United States by Sicilian organized crime members who used pizza parlors as fronts. Following the investigation, Director Freeh served as the Federal Govern-ment principal courtroom attorney in the 14-month trial and won the conviction of 16 of 17 codefendants. In May, 1990, he was appointed a Special Prosecutor by the Attorney General to oversee the investigation into the mail-bomb murders, and in 1991, former President George Bush appointed Director Freeh a United States Dis-trict Court Judge for the Southern District of New York. On July 20, 1993, he was nominated Director of the FBI by President Bill Clinton. He was confirmed by the U.S. Senate and was sworn in as Director on September 1, 1993.

Director Freeh has received several awards for his exemplary accomplish-ments, which include investigations and prosecutions relating to racketeering, drugs, organized crime, fraud, and terrorism.

FRANK J. GUARINI
United States Representative - Chairman NIAF

United States Representative Frank J. Guarini was born on August 20, 1924 in Jersey City, N.J. He received his Bachelor of Arts degrees from New York University School of Law, and pursued advanced studies at the Hague Academy of International Law in the Netherlands. Later, he was admitted to the practice of law in New Jersey and before the United States Supreme Court, the U.S. Treasury Department, the U.S. Court of Appeals, the U.S. Tax Court, and the U.S. Court of International Trade.

In 1978, he was elected to the United States House of Representatives for New Jersey's 14 Congressional District, serving for seven terms. As a result of having served 12 years on the Trade Subcommittee of the House Ways and Means Committee, Congressman Guarini developed considerable expertise on trade matters. He was deeply involved in the enactment of the Free Trade Agreement with Canada, Israel and the proposed agreement with Mexico. When trade reform became an issue, Congressman Guarini worked hard to modernize our trade and tariff laws to make sure that other countries opened their markets just as U.S. has been providing open markets to others. Congressman Guarini was a Majority Whip At-Large for the Democratic Leadership Organization. While in Congress, he was a senior member of the Budget Committee, and served many years in the Select Committee on Narcotics Abuse.

Congressman Guarini is currently Chairman of the National Italian Foundation. He founded the Guarini Center for Government Affairs of St. Peter's College where he serves as a trustee. He also serves as a trustee of John Cabot University, Rome, Italy. He has written numerous articles and co-authored the book *New Jersey Rules of Evidence.*

VINCENT T. DEVITA, J.R.
Director - Yale Cancer Center

Dr. Vincent T. DeVita was born on March 7, 1935, the son of Isabelle LoNano and Vincent DeVita. He earned his Bachelor of Science degree from the College of William and Mary in 1957. He was awarded his M.D. degree with distinction from George Washington University School of Medicine in 1961, where he was also Professor of Medicine. Dr. DeVita spent the early part of his career at the National Cancer Institute (NCI) of the National Institutes of Health. In 1988, he joined Memorial Sloan-Kettering Cancer Center as Physician-In Chief, and Professor of Medicine at Cornell University School of Medicine until he returned to Yale in New Haven, CT, in 1993, where he is currently Director of the Yale Cancer Center and Professor of Medicine and Professor of Epidemiology and Public Health at the Yale School of Medicine. Dr. DeVita has had international recognition for his accomplishments. While at NCI, he was instrumental in developing combination chemotherapy programs that ultimately led to an effective regimen of curative chemotherapy of Hodgkin's disease and diffused large cell lymphomas. Along with colleagues at the NCI, he developed the four-drug combination, known by the acronym MOPP, that increased the cure-rate for patients with advanced Hodgkin's disease from nearly zero to over 70 percent. Dr. DeVita and his colleagues played a major role in the development of similar treatment for other lymphomas and cancers of the ovary and breast. Dr. DeVita serves on the editorial boards of numerous scientific journals and is the author and coauthor of more than 350 scientific articles. He is one of the three editors of *Cancer: Principles and Practice of Oncology, Biologic Therapy of Cancer*, a textbook on AIDS, and *The Cancer Journal from Scientific American*. He has received many awards including the Alessio Pazcoller Award and Medal of Honor.

GIOACCHINO LANZA TOMASI
Director of the Italian Cultural Institute of New York

Professor Gioacchino Lanza Tomasi, director of the Italian Cultural Institute of New York, was born in Rome in 1934, and followed his family to Palermo after the war. In 1957 he was adopted by Giuseppe Tomasi di Lampedusa, his distant cousin, to whom he had been particularly close. He is a professor of Music History at the University of Palermo, and has enjoyed a long association with the major opera houses of Italy as an artistic director. His scholarly work in musicology has focused primarily on stylistic analysis and reception studies of 19th century Italian opera and 20th century music. Professor Lanza Tomasi was one of the first to bring exponents of the American school to Italy, commissioning Morton Feldman's *Neither* to text by Samuel Beckett, Philip Glass and Robert Wilson's *The Civil Wars.* The artists whom he has commissioned to design productions for the Rome Opera include Michelangelo Pistoletto *Neither,* and Mario Ceroli Paul Hindemith's *Sancta Susanna.* In 1970 he was appointed head of music history at the University of Salerno and in 1980 he became a full professor. Since 1983, he has been a professor of Music History at the University of Palermo, and until his appointment in New York he has been Chairman of the Education Department. In 1965 he began his work as a music organizer and gradually became the artistic director of various musical institutions, among which, the Rome Philharmonic Academy, and The Teatro Massimo of Palermo, the Teatro Opera of Rome. Professor Lanza Tomasi was the general director of the Roma Europa Arte e Cultura Foundation, and consultant on the reconstruction of the Vittorio Emanuele Theater of Messina. In the early years of his career he published various works on art history, specializing in Sicilian architecture, and later dedicating himself entirely to music criticism and management.

1982 - Cardinal Anthony Bevilacqua of Philadelphia, welcomes President Ronald Reagan.

TONY LO BIANCO
Actor

Tony Lo Bianco was born in Brooklyn, New York, the son of Sally and Carmelo Lo Bianco. After attending the Dramatic Work Shop Acting School in Manhattan, he went on quickly to a long successful career, distinguishing himself not only by the variety of roles he has brought to life, but also by the scope of his work. During his career, he has received numerous credits and awards for acting in films, television movies and mini-series, as well as in the theater. Mr. Lo Bianco produced the Broadway play *Hizzoner, the Life of Fiorello La Guardia* and earned an Emmy for his one-man show, an Obie for Best Actor in an off-Broadway production with *Yanks 3 Detroit 0 Top of the 7th,* and the Oscar Critics Circle Award for outstanding performance in *A View from the Bridge,* which also garnered him a Tony nomination. As a dramatic screen actor, Mr. Lo Bianco became widely recognized, and achieved prominence worldwide with the films, *The Honeymoon Killers*, Oscar Winning *The French Connection, Bloodbrother* with Richard Gere, Norman Jewison's, *City Heat* with Clint Eastwood and Burt Reynolds, Oliver Stone's *Nixon* with Anthony Hopkins, *The Juror, Tyson*, with George C. Scott, and *the Seven-Ups* with Roy Scheider. Mr. Lo Bianco has also left his mark on television with acclaimed performances in epic mini-series such as *Marco Polo, Jesus of Nazareth* and many others. Mr. Lo Bianco is also a talented director and producer. He has directed various stage productions and television programs. He served as artistic director for New York's Triangle Theater which he co-founded. Known for his humanitarian endeavors, Mr. Lo Bianco is the National Spokesperson for the Order Sons of Italy in America and uses his free time to raise funds for children's charities and community causes.

ANDREA MANTINEO
President and Editor of National Italian Daily *America Oggi*

Andrea Mantineo was born in Messina, Italy on January 20, 1942, the son of Francesco Mantineo and Angela Renda. After graduating from the Liceo Scientifico Sequenza in Messina and spending a year in Kenosha, Wisconsin, as an exchange student at St. Joseph High School, he studied Political Science at Messina University, while working as a reporter and page editor at *Tribuna del Mezzogiorno* daily paper. In 1970, Mr. Mantineo was hired by Fortunate Pope, then editor and publisher of *Il Progresso Italo-Americano,* as an assistant managing editor. Two years later he became managing editor and was appointed editor of the newspaper in 1981, when it was bought by an Italian publishing company. In 1988, after a bitter labor struggle, Il Progresso fired without severance, all its unionized workers. Mr. Mantineo and most of the former employees of il Progresso, pooling together their small financial resources, formed a corporation, Gruppo Editoriale Oggi, of which each one of them owns an equal share. They published the first issue of *America Oggi* on November 14, 1988 and in four months drove *Il Progresso* out of business. In a few years, *America Oggi* has established itself as the only voice of the Italian community in America. The newspaper is circulated in every east coast state and also reaches other areas with significant Italian communities.

Mr. Mantineo has been a member the Italian National Order of Professional Journalists since 1965, he is active in the Italian-American community, and is a member and past president of COMITES of New Jersey. Mr. Mantineo has been the recipient of numerous professional and community awards in the United States and in Italy. He resides in Emerson, New Jersey with his wife and his 28-year-old daughter Daniela.

YOGI BERRA
Baseball Player - Hall of Fame

Lawrence Peter "Yogi" Berra was born on May 12, 1925 in St. Louis, MO. and grew up on Elizabeth Street in a neighborhood called *The Hill*. He got his nickname from a childhood friend. In 1942, Mr. Berra was playing minor league ball and was approached by the then Cardinal General Manager, Branch Rickey. He turned down Richey's offer and was signed up later by Yankees Scout Leo Brown. He was assigned to the Norfolk Tars of the Class B Piedmont League. During a double header, Mr. Berra had perhaps his most productive game ever. That day, he was credited with driving in 23 runs. At the age of 18 he joined the Navy and participated in the D-Day invasion at Omaha Beach, served in North Africa and Italy, and then was finally stationed back in the States. After the war, Mr. Berra returned to baseball and became a 15-time All Star, winning the American League Most Valuable Player three times, in 1951, 54 and 55. He played in 14 World Series and holds numerous World Series records including most games by a catcher (63), hits (71), and times on a winning team (10), first in at bats, first in doubles, second in RBI's, third in home runs and BOB's. Mr. Berra also hit the first pinch hit home run in World Series history in 1947. Mr. Berra was named Yankees Manager in 1964 and went on to win the AL pennant. In 1972, he was named Met Manager, and the following year brought the Mets from last place in the final month of the season to win the National League pennant. In 1976, he returned to the Yankees as a coach. George Steinbrenner later hired him to manage the Yankees. In 1986, he signed on as a coach with the Houston Astros, and remained with them until his retirement in 1992. Mr. Berra is one of only a few managers to have won pennants in both American and National Leagues. He was elected to the National Baseball Hall of Fame in 1972.

JOSEPH A. ZACCAGNINO
President and CEO Yale-New Haven Hospital

Joseph A. Zaccagnino was born 1946 in New Rochelle, New York, son of Helen Tridico and Joseph Zaccagnino. He joined Yale-New Haven Hospital as an administrative resident in 1970 and held various senior management positions until he was named executive vice president and chief operating officer in 1978.

In 1991, he was appointed president and chief executive officer of Yale- New Haven Hospital and the Yale-New Haven Health System, which is the parent corporation for Yale-New Haven Hospital, Bridgeport Hospital and, pending regulatory approval, Greenwich Hospital.

Mr. Zaccagnino received his undergraduate degree from the University of Connecticut at Storrs and a master's degree in public health in hospital administration from Yale University School of Medicine in New Haven, Connecticut. He serves on the boards of National Committee for Quality Health Care, Connecticut United for Research Excellence and the New Haven Savings Bank. He also serves on the New Haven Regional Leadership Council and the Tweed New Haven Airport Authority.

Mr. Zaccagnino is also a member of the American College of Healthcare Executives, the Hospital Research and Development Institute, the American Hospital Association and the Healthcare Executive's Study Society.

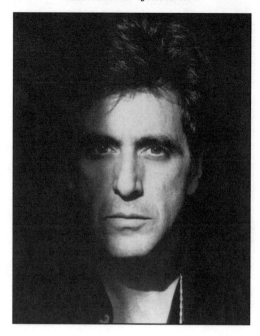

AL PACINO
Actor and Director

Al Pacino has had a very successful acting career, and is today one of the world's most popular actors. He is an eight-time Academy Award nominee. After having received four Best Actor nominations for ... *Justice For All, The Godfather Part II, Dog Day Afternoon* and *Serpico*, which also earned him a Golden Globe Award, Mr. Pacino finally won an Oscar for Best Actor for his outstanding performance as Lt. Colonel Frank Slade in Universal's *Scent Of A Woman,* for which he also won a Golden Globe Award. He was nominated three other times: as Best Supporting Actor for his role as Michael Corleone in *The Godfather;* he also won a 1990 American Comedy Award for his role as Big Boy Caprice in Dick Tracy, and in David Mamet's screen adaptation of *Glengarry Glen Ross.* As a child growing up in the Bronx, he would re-create for his mother and grandparents the characters he saw in movies. His grammar school teachers encouraged him to apply to the famed High School of Performing Arts, which he attended while working part-time as a theatre usher. After studying with Herbert Berghof and later with Lee Strasberg at the Actor's Studio, Mr. Pacino made his professional acting debut in the off-Broadway production of *The Connection* and *Hello, Out There.* He won an Obie Award for Israel Horovitz's *The Indian Wants The Bronx.* Mr. Pacino's other films include *The Godfather Part III, Scarface, Serpico, Bobby Deerfield* and *Scarecrow,* for which he received the Best Actor Award at the Cannes Film Festival in 1973. He made his film debut in 1971 in *The Panic In Needle Park.* Mr. Pacino directed and starred in Eugene O'Neill's *Hughie* which opened in early July 1996 at the Long Wharf Theater in New Haven. He also produced, starred in and co-directed the independent film adaptation of the play *The Local Stigmatic.*

The Verrazzano Bridge, Staten Island - The bridge was named in honor of the Florentine explorer Giovanni Da Verrazzano, discoverer of New York Harbor in 1524. John La Corte, an Italian immigrant, and president of the Italian Historical Society of Brooklyn, led the fight for 10 years to have the bridge named for the Italian navigator. The bridge opened on November 21, 1964. Governor Rockefeller of New York, later, with Governor Meyner of N.J., Governor Glauson of Maine, Governor Del Sesto of R.I., and Governor Luther Hodges of N.C., proclaimed April 17 Verrazzano Day. The First Verrazzano Day proclamation was presented to Mr. La Corte in 1957 by the Governor of N.J., Robert B. Meyner.

1999 - Mayor of New York, Rudolph Giuliani, at a press conference, displays a new sign after proposing the renaming of a portion of the West Side Highway as a lasting tribute to Joe DiMaggio.

JOSEPH TUSIANI
Professor of Italian Literature - Author and Poet

Joseph Tusiani, Distinguished Service Professor, was born in San Marco in Lamis, (Foggia) in the Apulian region. He came to the United States of America in 1947, and taught Italian Literature for thirty-five years in several universities. He retired in 1983 from the City University of New York. He is a very well known translator of Italian poetry; among his most famous books are *The Complete Poems of Michelangelo*, Tasso's *Jerusalem Delivered* and *Creation of the World,* Boccaccio's *Nymphs of Fiesole,* Dante's *Lyric Poems*, Pulci's *Morgante and Leopardi's Canti*. His Leopardi translation has been reissued on the occasion of the bicentennial of the poet's birth with the sponsorship of the Centro Studi Leopardiani di Recanati. In his three voluminous anthologies, *The Age of Dante, Italian Poets of the Renaissance,* and *From Marino to Marinetti,* he has introduced nearly 150 Italian poets to the English-speaking world. A poet in his own right, Professor Tusiani is the author of *Rind and All The Fifth Season,* and *Gente Mia and Other Poems.* He is also the author of a play in verse, *If Gold Should Rust*, which won the *Alice Fay Di Castagnola Award* of the Poetry Society of America in 1969. He also published six collections of verse in Latin, and two volumes of *Carmina Latina*. One of the best-known Italian American authors, Professor Tusiani has greatly contributed to ethnic literature with his autobiographical trilogy: *La Parola Difficile, la Parola Nuova* and *La Parola Antica*. In addition, he is also the author of seven volumes of poetry in his Gargano dialect. His literary production has been the subject of eight doctoral dissertations in various Italian universities. Professor Tusiani is the recipient of the first Fiorello La Guardia Award. In 1963 President John F. Kennedy invited him to record his poetry for the Archives of the Library of Congress.

MARY CIVIELLO
Journalist - TV News Anchor

Mary Civiello was born and raised in Kansas City, Missouri. She earned a master's and bachelor's degree from the University of Missouri-Columbia.

Ms. Civiello is a six time Emmy Award journalist with 20 years experience in television news. She appears weekly as the *Family Money* correspondent for WCBS-TV, the CBS flagship station in New York City. Ms. Civiello also anchors the news for CNBC-TV, NBC's cable TV business station, and has started a media training business, Civiello Communication Group.

For 15 years, up until 1998, Ms. Civiello reported, and for several years, anchored the top rated morning news for WNBC-TV, New York. Her Emmy Awards include two for anchoring live coverage of breaking news stories, others for an investigative health feature and spot news reporting.

Ms. Civiello is a member of Sigma Delta Chi, a professional journalists association. Sigma Delta Chi awarded her their prestigious Deadline Club Award for her investigation of a Bronx school district. Her investigation helped lead to the arrest and conviction of two board members on corruption charges. Prior to coming to New York, Ms. Civiello reported and anchored in Eau Claire, WI, Portland, Oregon, San Jose, California and Hartford, Connecticut. While at WFSB-TV in Hartford, she traveled to Italy twice to report on the damage done by the earthquake of November 1980, and later to chronicle the ties many Italian Americans in Connecticut maintain to their homeland.

New Haven - St. Michael Church, the first Italian Church in Connecticut,
was dedicated in October 1889.

Father Michael Tarro, C.S.
Pastor

RICHARD A. GRASSO

Chairman and Chief Executive Officer of the New York Stock Exchange

Richard A. Grasso was born in Jackson Heights, Queens. He has been chairman and chief executive officer of the New York Stock Exchange (NYSE) since June 1, 1995. His grandfather Fortunato Casagrande arrived in the United States in 1886, at the age of four.

Mr. Grasso joined the NYSE in 1968, rising steadily through the ranks, he was president and chief operating officer since June of 1988 and became executive vice chairman of the Exchange on January 1, 1991. He is the first member of the NYSE staff to be elected to any of these positions in the Exchange's 206-year history.

During his tenure, Mr. Grasso has assigned the highest priorities to assuring the NYSE's position as a premier global equities market; enhancing the Exchange's competitive edge by applying cutting-edge technology to trading, regulatory and administrative operations; and upholding the NYSE's bedrock corporate values, starting with integrity and embracing excellence, respect for individual and a customer-comes-first orientation. He is chairman of the YMCA of Greater New York and a member of the boards of directors of the Centurion Foundation and New York City Police Foundation. In January 1997, New York City Mayor Rudolph Giuliani appointed him as co-chairman of project Smart Schools, a program designed to provide computers for New York City classrooms and computer training for teachers. In November of 1997, the mayor appointed Mr. Grasso to the board of directors of New York City Public Private Initiatives, Inc. For the past six years, he has served as honorary chairman of the friends of the Statue of Liberty National Monument-Ellis Island Foundation.

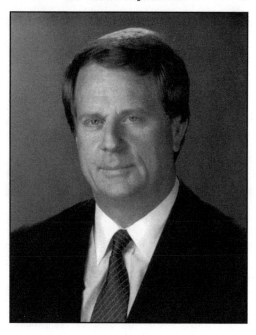

MICHAEL J. ADANTI
President - Southern Connecticut State University

Michael J. Adanti's appointment in 1984 as President of Southern Connecticut State University marked the culmination of a long and productive career at the university that saw him go from an undergraduate in 1959, to football captain in 1962, to graduate student in 1970, to president in 1984.

Born in 1940, Mr. Adanti graduated from Southern in the class of '63, earning a Bachelor of Science degree in Elementary Education and Science. Following graduation, in 1966, he was awarded a Master of Science degree in Student Personnel from the University of Bridgeport and, shortly afterward, was named Assistant Dean of students at Southern.

From 1977-1979, Mr. Adanti served as Southern's first Dean of Personnel Administration. Before being named president, he was called upon twice — as chief executive officer/executive vice president and as acting president — to lead the university through difficult times.

But his appointment as president was a first. It made him the first Southern Connecticut State University graduate to become president of his alma mater, and the first Southern graduate to become president of any university.

Mr. Adanti was a two-term mayor of Ansonia, Connecticut, from 1973-1977. In 1976, he ran as the democratic candidate for the U.S. House of Representatives from the 5th Congressional District.

New York - 1998 - At a reception of the Italian Welfare League, from left are:
Mrs. Claudia Massimo Berns, assistant to Governor Pataki for Italian Affairs; Ms. Joan Migliori;
Consul General of Italy, Giorgio Radicati; Giuliana Ridolfi Cardillo,
Press Officer, Istituto Italiano di Cultura, New York.

Newark, N.J. - Publisher Ace Alagna with Connie Francis, the first woman to
be selected as Grand Marshal of the Columbus Day Parade.

FRANK STELLA
CEO of The F.D. Stella Products Co. - Former Chairman NIAF

Frank Stella is founder, chairman and CEO of The F.D. Stella Products Company, Detroit, designers and distributors of food service and dining equipment. He founded the company in 1946, and today leads a network of affiliates serving markets in Michigan and throughout the United States. Mr. Stella is also Chairman and CEO of Stella International, New York, a consulting, joint venture and importing firm, and a member of the board of directors of Metropolitan Realty Corporation. An alumnus of the University of Detroit College of Commerce and Finance, Mr. Stella has devoted his life to the betterment of others. He has been a supporter of education, healthcare and business. Among the many business organizations benefitting from his involvement, the Federal Home Loan Bank of Indianapolis, the Greater Detroit Chamber of Commerce, the Economic Alliance for Michigan and the Economic Club of Detroit. In 1997, he was named in Michigan, Michigander of the year. From 1992 to 1999, Mr. Stella was Chairman of the National Italian Foundation of Washington, D.C., and has served as board member for many medical and educational institutions including the University of Detroit, Mt. Carmel Mercy Hospital and Sacred Heart Rehabilitation Center. He is vice chairman of Detroit Symphony Orchestra Hall, and Michigan Opera Theater. In World War II, Mr. Stella was drafted as a private, and was honorably discharged as a Major in the U.S. Air Force.

He was decorated by the government of Italy three times and received it's highest decoration, *Grande Ufficiale*. He was awarded a doctorate in Business by Gentium Pacem University in Rome and Cleary College. By the rector of the University of Bologna, he received the Seal of the university.

LAWRENCE J. DE NARDIS
President - University of New Haven

Dr. Lawrence J. De Nardis has served as president of the University of New Haven, Connecticut, since 1991. He is a former U.S. Congressman and Professor of Political Science who has had a distinguished career in education and government.

Dr. De Nardis holds a Ph.D. degree in Political Science from New York University and a Bachelor's degree in Economics from Holy Cross. His academic experience includes nearly two decades of teaching at Albertus Magnus College, Yale University and the University of New Haven. He was also a guest scholar at the Woodrow Wilson International Center for Scholars of the Smithsonian Institution in Washington, D.C.

In the field of government, Dr. De Nardis has had the rare distinction of serving as both a federal and state legislator. He was elected to the U.S. House of Representatives from Connecticut's Third District in 1980, and was chosen as one of the outstanding freshmen in the 97th Congress. He served on the Education Committee on Narcotics Abuse and Control. He had previously served five terms as a state senator in Connecticut from 1971-79, where he was Chairman of the Finance Committee, Program Review Committee and Deputy Minority Leader. In 1985 and 1986, he also served as Assistant Secretary for Legislation at the U.S. Department of Health and Human Services. In addition, in 1990, he was appointed by Governor Lowell P. Weicker as Chairman of the Connecticut Board of Governors of Higher Education. He also served as a member of the Board of Regents of the National Library of Medicine, appointed by former President George Bush.

GAETANO CIANCIO
Transplant Surgeon - University of Miami

Dr. Gaetano Ciancio was born in Roccapiemonte (Salerno), Italy. He arrived in the United States full of enthusiasm and hope, not knowing the multiple difficulties that a foreign medical doctor goes through trying to enter the American medical community. After spending two years in research in molecular biology and flow cytometry at the Veteran Administration Medical Center (Miami - Florida), he was accepted in the residency surgical program at Jackson Memorial Hospital. Here he finished general surgery, and did four more years in urology.

In 1991, Dr. Ciancio developed the first technique to analyze DNA and nuclear protein in paraffin-embedded tissue from different cancers. This technique is presently being used at M.D. Anderson Cancer Center (Texas), to analyze tumors (bladder, prostate, and others), with the objective of trying to understand tumor clinical behavior and to improve treatment. In 1992, he performed and published the first radical prostatectomy for prostate cancer in a heart transplant patient. Later in 1994, he published the first series of renal parenchymal-sparing for renal cell carcinoma performed at the University of Miami. Dr. Ciancio, in 1993, was accepted in the transplant fellowship of the Division Transplantation at the University of Miami. He is the first in the history of the Jackson Memorial Hospital residency training program who entered the field of transplantation, and was trained by Dr. Joshua Miller, currently president of the American Society of Transplant Surgeons. On December 31, 1994, he was one of the two surgeons that performed the first adult intestinal transplant in the southeast of the United States. In July of 1995, he was one of the doctors of the American team who saved the life of a patient after a multivisceral transplantation of six organs (the first in the world). The surgery lasted 36 hours.

ACE ALAGNA
Publisher of the *Italian Tribune News*

Ace Alagna was born on February 17, 1925, in Newark, New Jersey, the son of Marianne Barbieri Alagna and Mario Alagna. His parents emigrated to the United States from Italy in 1900. Mr. Alagna has been the owner/publisher of the *Italian Tribune News* for 30 years. He was a member of the White House Press Corps, and he was assigned to five United States presidents, including Harry Truman, Dwight Eisenhower, John F. Kennedy, Lyndon Johnson, and Richard Nixon. For nearly three decades, Mr. Alagna and his newspaper have been the sole sponsors of the Columbus Day Parade in Newark. He has brought to Newark's "Little Italy" some of the nation's most distinguished celebrities: Joe DiMaggio, Bob and Dolores (DeFini) Hope, Tony Bennett, Tommy LaSorda, and Connie Francis. In addition, awards for outstanding service on behalf of the Italian American community have been bestowed by Mr. Alagna upon such personalities as Frank Sinatra, George Bush, and Jimmy Carter. In 1988, he was asked by the White House to host a Columbus Day celebration in New Jersey for President Ronald Reagan. More than 3,500 Italian Americans witnessed in West Orange, Mr. Alagna's presentation of the Columbus Bronze Award to the president. In 1976, he established the Italian Tribune News Earthquake Relief Fund to help raise more than one million dollars in relief funds. The money was used to built a children's day care center in Udine, northern Italy. Four years later, when another earthquake devastated the region of Campania, Italy, the Relief Fund raised more than two million dollars in donations, and another children's daycare center was erected in Palomonte. Mr. Alagna has been the recipient of numerous honors and awards throughout his illustrious career, among which are the Boys Towns of Italy Humanitarian Award, and the 1991 Gold Medal of Honor from UNICO.

JENO F. PAULUCCI

Founder of the National Italian American Foundation

Jeno F. Paulucci was born on July 7, 1918 in Aurora, Minnesota, the son of Ettore e Nicolina Burati from Bellisio Sulfare, Pesaro. In the 1940's, he borrowed $2,500 to start the production of American-Oriental foods in Minnesota. Twenty years later he sold the nationally dominant Chun King Corporation for $63 million cash to R.J. Reynolds Tobacco. As it's first chairman, he then helped form and operate RJR. Food, Inc., now the RJR Nabisco giant.

Mr. Paulucci built his Wilderness pie filling business to national prominence, and invested in the worldwide Cornelius Company, where as chairman he revitalized the firm's market position and sold both companies at their prime. His famous "Jeno's Pizza Rolls" rocketed Jeno's Inc., to national leadership before he sold it to The Pillsbury Company. Then he created Heathrow, a new city in Florida.

Recently, Mr. Paulucci started two more national companies, Luigino's Pasta Lovers and Steak House, a prototype casual Italian restaurant and Luigino Inc. where he produces frozen entrees and snacks under the Michelina's brand (his mother's name) and Yu Sing brand frozen Oriental entrees and snacks.

Known to be a crusader for the common man, Mr. Paulucci is dedicated to the responsibilities of business. He and his family gave more than $2 million in gifts to employees upon sale of Chun King, and the Jeno and Lois Paulucci Family Foundation is noted for its philanthropy.

Mr. Paulucci was the founder of the National Italian American Foundation, in Washington, D.C. He was its National Chairman during 17 years of development as a strong voice for the nation's 25 million Italian Americans.

1979 - From left to right: former New York Yankee scout Ed Liberatore;
son-in-law of Ace Alagna and former New Jersey Assemblyman Buddy Fortunato;
New York Yankee Hall of Famer Joe DiMaggio; and *Italian Tribune News* publisher Ace Alagna.

1989 - Ace Alagna, executive director of the Columbus Day Parade,
with Grand Marshal and longtime friend Tommy LaSorda.

FRANCESCO PAOLO FULCI
Ambassador of Italy - United Nations

Ambassador Francesco Paolo Fulci was born in Messina, Italy, on March 19, 1931. He earned his Law Degree *cum Laude* at the University of Messina. Later, as a Fulbright Scholar, he received a Master's degree in Comparative Law at Columbia University in New York. In 1955 he received the Diploma of the Hague Academy of International Law, and attended the College of Europe in Bruges, on Italian Government scholarship.

Ambassador Fulci, a career diplomat, began the Italian foreign service on November 12, 1956. He was promoted to the rank of Ambassador on November 21, 1986. Previously, he served as Vice-Consul at the Consulate General of Italy in New York, and was also Assistant to Honorable Gaetano Martino, former Foreign Minister, Chief of the Italian Delegation to the XV General Assembly of the United Nations. From 1980 to 1985, he was Ambassador of Italy in Ottawa. Later, on to Bruxelles (NATO), as Ambassador and Permanent Representative of Italy to the North Atlantic Council in Brussels.

Since 1882, several members of his family served as members of the Italian Parliament. His father served as a member of the Chamber of Deputies for two consecutive legislatures in the post-World War II period. During his career, Ambassador Fulci received numerous honors and awards, among which, the Cross of Merit of the Federal Republic of Germany, Commander of the Imperial Order of the Rising Sun of Japan, Knight Great Cross of the Order Francisco de Miranda of Venezuela. He is also a recipient of three Honorary Doctorates in Law from the University of Windsor, Ontario, St. Thomas Aquinas College, New York, and St. John's University, New York.

CAMILLO RICORDI
Chief of the Division of Cellular Transplantation - Surgery

Dr. Camillo Ricordi was born on April 1,1957. He concluded his post graduate studies and his surgical residency at the University of Milan with the highest scores and honors. After medical school and serving in the Italian Air Force (Lieutenant), Dr. Ricordi received a Research Trainee Award from the National Institute of Health and was a Research Associate at Washington University in St. Louis. In 1988 he returned to Milano to serve as Attending Surgeon at San Raffaele Institute, University of Milan School of Medicine, and he then spent four years as Associate Professor of Surgery and Director of Cellular Transplantation at the University of Pittsburgh Transplantation Institute. Since 1953, he has been working at the University of Miami, and now serves as the Stacy Joy Goodman Professor of Surgery and Medicine and Chief of the Division of Cellular Transplantation, Department of Surgery, at the University of Miami School of Medicine. Since September of 1996, he also assumed the position of Scientific Director and Chief Academic Officer of the Diabetes Research Institute, at the same university.

Dr. Ricordi is well known for inventing the machine that made it possible to isolate large numbers of islet cells (insulin-producing cells) from the human pancreas and for performing the first series of clinical islet transplants that reversed diabetes after implantation of donor purified islet into the liver of recipients with diabetes. The procedure in now used by laboratories performing clinical islet transplants worldwide. From 1992 to 1994, Dr. Ricordi was the president of the Cell Transplant Society. He has received various honors, awards and Research Grant Awards from the Juvenile Diabetes Foundation and the American Diabetes Association.

ORLANDO PELLICCIA, Jr.
Chief of Surgery - St. Raphael's Hospital

Dr. Orlando Pelliccia was born in New Haven, Connecticut, March 21, 1913, son of Orlando and Rose Verdi Pelliccia. He attended public schools in New Haven, graduated from Yale University in 1935, and the Johns Hopkins School of Medicine in 1939.

After completing his residency in general surgery at Union Memorial Hospital in Baltimore, Dr. Pelliccia joined Dr. Verdi in the private practice of surgery at St. Raphael's Hospital in New Haven, Connecticut. He was the nephew of Dr. William F. Verdi, St. Raphael's first Chief of Surgery, after whom the Verdi Memorial Building at the hospital complex is named.

At St. Raphael's, Dr. Pelliccia served as Chief of Surgery from 1953 to 1961, he later served as Acting Chairman, and then Chairman of the Department of Surgery until the early 1980's. He was a clinical associate professor of surgery at the Yale Medical School, as well as a member of the American College of Surgeons and the New England Surgical Society. He was also fellow at the American College of Surgeons, and a member of the American Medical Association.

Dr. Pelliccia died July 3, 1989 at the hospital after a brief illness. At the time of his death, he had maintained his private practice with his associate Dr. Venkatachala Sreenivas, another prominent surgeon in New Haven.

1999 - Luisa De Lauro, mother of Congresswoman Rosa De Lauro, is the longest serving member of the New Haven Board of Aldermen. Mrs. De Lauro and her daughter, Congresswoman Rosa De Lauro, were honored with the Distinguished Service Award, by the Italian-American Historical Society of New Haven. From left to right, sitting: Mr. Phil Paolella, founder of the society; Luisa De Lauro and Professor Michael Vena, president of the society. Standing, from left to right: Congresswoman Rosa De Lauro and Dr. Larry Pisani, past president of the society.

The New Haven Colony Historical Society, located on Whitney Avenue, New Haven, Connecticut. The society is a private, non-profit educational institution established in 1862 to preserve the cultural history of Greater New Haven. The building was built in 1929 to house the collection of the New Haven Colony Historical Society, and was designed by J. Frederick Kelly.

JOSEPH MASELLI

Founder of the American Italian Foundation Museum and Research Library

Joseph Maselli was born on May 30, 1924 in Newark, New Jersey, the son of Mary Iannetti and Frank Maselli from Foggia, Italy. He earned a Bachelor of Arts degree at Tulane University in three years while working as a Public Accountant. A long-time New Orleans resident, Mr. Maselli is the founder and Chief Executive Officer of one of the largest distributing companies in the New Orleans area. He developed the internationally famous *Piazza d'Italia* with the City of New Orleans, and is currently working to develop property adjacent to that site. In addition to many other business activities, he developed apartment complexes and shopping centers, and owned and managed the successful *Italian Village of the Louisiana World Exposition.* Mr. Maselli has been the catalyst for countless Louisiana Italian-American activities, founding the first state wide organization of Italian Americans that later became the American Italian Federation of the Southeast with over 9,000 members in five states, Louisiana, Mississippi, Alabama, Georgia and Texas. He later founded the American Italian Renaissance Foundation Museum and Research Library, to honor Louisiana Italian-Americans who have excelled in athletics, he founded the Louisiana American Italian Sports Hall of Fame. Mr. Maselli has been a member of many civic, academic, and charitable organizations. In 1992, the Governor of Louisiana appointed him chairman of the Louisiana Quincentennial Commission. He brought to New Orleans the three famous Spanish Caravels, la Nina, La Pinta, e la Santa Maria, enabling many people, including children, to experience the history of a major event of the fifteenth century that changed the world forever. He also organized significant responses to several earthquakes in Italy, rebuilding Venzone's City Hall, and Laviano's Children's Medical Center.

ANCHOR LINE
MEDITERRANEAN SERVICE
PROPOSED SAILINGS
FROM
NAPLES and PALERMO
TO
NEW YORK
(SUBJECT TO CHANGE)

S. S.				FROM NAPLES		FROM PALERMO	
PERUGIA	-	-	-	Mar. 5, 1914		Mar. 6, 1914	
ITALIA	-	-	-	Mar. 26, "		Mar. 27, "	
CALABRIA	-	-	-	April 9, "		April 10, "	
PERUGIA	-	-	-	April 30, "		May 1, "	
ITALIA	-	-	-	May 14, "		May 15, "	
CALABRIA	-	-	-	June 4, "		June 5, "	
PERUGIA	-	-	-	June 25, "		June 26, "	

THIRD-CLASS PASSAGE RATES
PREPAID
BY ALL STEAMERS

FROM
NAPLES, PALERMO OR MESSINA

Per Adult
$33.00
Children over 5 years and under 10, half fare.
Over 1 year and under 5, quarter fare.
Infants free.

ORIENTAL POINTS

FROM					FROM				
Piraeus	to New York	-	$37.50		Jaffa	to New York	-	-	$45.50
Patras	" " "	-	38.50		Beyrouth	" " "	-	-	46.50
Alexandria	" " "	-	43.50						

Infants under 1 year, $2.00. Children between 1 and 3 years, half of ocean fare, Naples to New York. Children between 3 and 12 years, half of through fare from Oriental points.

NOTE—RATE FROM PIRAEUS DOES NOT INCLUDE FOOD TO NAPLES.

These Steamships are fitted with **MARCONI WIRELESS TELEGRAPH** and lighted throughout by **ELECTRICITY.** Excellent accommodations and good service.

21—24 State St., New York, Feb. 19, 1914.
HENDERSON BROTHERS, General Agents.

COMPLIMENTS OF JOSEPH MASELLI

New Orleans
1994 - Steamship company ad indicating Mediterranean proposed sailings and charges from Naples and Palermo, Italy, to New York during the biggest immigration period.

1996 - The Mayor of Norwalk, Connecticut, Frank J. Esposito, with the Governor of Connecticut, John G. Rowland, at the Mayor's Golf Tourney. Mayor Esposito, former Commissioner of the Norwalk Housing Authority, was elected mayor of the City of Norwalk in 1987, and has since been re-elected for six consecutive terms.

1999 - The Governor of Connecticut, John G. Rowland, with the Mayor of New York, Rudolph Giuliani, greeting people at the Prescott Bush Award Dinner.

New Orleans - Piazza D'Italia

CHRIS DE PINO

State Representative - Chairman of the Republican Party

Chris De Pino was born in New Haven, Connecticut, on July 10, 1952. He graduated from Notre Dame High School, attended Southern Connecticut State University and received an Associate's degree in Education from South Central Community College in New Haven. He also attended the Polytechnic Institute in New York for urban mass transportation planning, receiving a fellowship from the Federal Transportation Administration.

Mr. De Pino was first elected to the Connecticut House of Representatives in a special election in February 1992. He was reelected in November of both 1992 and 1994 to continue serving the 97th District of New Haven. He is a Republican in a city with a Democrat to Republican registration of 9 to 1. In the General Assembly, Mr. De Pino serves as Ranking Member of the Public Safety Committee and also serves on the Transportation Committee.

On January 23, 1996, State Representative Chris De Pino was elected Chairman of the Republican State Central Committee. He was elected with the approval and guidance of Governor John G. Rowland.

Mr. De Pino served on the New Haven Board of Aldermen from 1989 to 1993 and was a minority leader on that panel. For over 20 years, he worked for Metro-North Commuter Railroad as a train conductor and transportation manager. He received the President's Club Award from Metro-North for excellence in his job. In addition, he studies music and plays the harmonica.

New Orleans - 1978 - Dedication of "Piazza D'Italia." From left to right: Joseph C. Canizzaro, land owner; Joseph Maselli, president American Italian Federation; Mayor "Dutch" Morial; Steve Dwyer, attorney, and Jerome Camiola, committee member.

New Orleans
1978 - A local Italian-American band plays at the dedication of Piazza D'Italia.

JOSEPH A. ZAGAME
Philatelist

Joseph A. Zagame was born in Stromboli, one of the seven Eolie Islands, where Roberto Rossellini and Ingrid Bergman made the classic movie *Stromboli*. In 1955, he came to Brooklyn from Italy to join his parents Liberatore Zagame and Caterina Tesoriero. Dr. Zagame graduated from the Liceo Classico in Milazzo, Sicily, and holds a Ph.D. in Business Administration from the University of Messina, Italy. His passion to collect stamps began at the age of 12, while attending the Gymnasium in Castroreale, Messina. In America, Dr. Zagame became a pioneer of Philately. He proposed to the Postmaster General of the United States the issue of many special slogan cancellations, and commemorative stamps honoring great Italian immigrants who contributed to the development of America. Commemorative stamps and special cancellations proposed by Dr. Zagame and issued by the Postmaster General include: Filippo Mazzei, Enrico Caruso, Arturo Toscanini, Enrico Fermi, Cesare Beccaria, Antonio Meucci, Maria Montessori, Joe Petrosino, Cristoforo Colombo, Madre Cabrini and Guglielmo Marconi.

The Postmaster General of Italy, in 1975, issued a stamp proposed by Dr. Zagame, dedicated to the "Italian Emigration in the World." Later, he suggested a stamp that was issued with the reproduction of Stromboli, his place of birth.

Dr. Zagame is the founder of the Italy Philatelic Society in America and is Chairman of the Culture Committee of the Tri-State Congress. In 1988, he received the Congressional Medal of Merit, and in 1993, he received the Italian civil decoration: Commendatore della Repubblica Italiana, conferred by the President of Italy Oscar Luigi Scalfaro. He was also awarded a Honorary Doctorate from the Costantinian University in Rhode Island.

PAUL CELLUCCI
Governor - Massachusetts

Governor Paul Cellucci, a native of Massachusetts, received his law degree from Boston College Law School in 1973. In 1970, he graduated from the Boston School of Management, where he served in the Reserve Officers Training Corps (ROTC). He also served in the U.S. Army Reserves from 1970 until 1978, when he was honorably discharged with the rank of Captain.

His career in government began in 1970 when he was elected to the Hudson Charter Commission. One year later, he won a seat on the Hudson Board of Selectmen and he served on that panel until 1977. In 1976 he was elected to the first of four terms in the Massachusetts House of Representatives. In 1984, Governor Cellucci was elected to the Massachusetts Senate from the Middlesex and Worcester District. During his third Senate term he became the Assistant Republican Leader.

On November 3, 1998, he was elected Governor of Massachusetts on a ticket with Lieutenant Governor Jane Swift. He had been serving as Governor since July 1997 when Bill Weld resigned the post. Previously he was also elected Lieutenant Governor in 1990 on a ticket with former Governor Bill Weld.

Governor Cellucci, a strong advocate for smaller government and lower taxes, offered a major cut in the Massachusetts income tax on his first day as Governor. He has also been a leader in education reform, access to health care, and the fight against domestic violence.

In the private sector Governor Cellucci has had 30 years experience in working with his family's auto dealership, and 17 years practicing law, serving as a partner in the Hudson law firm of Kittredge, Cellucci and Moreira.

STEPHEN H. ACUNTO
President of CINN - Publisher of *La Follia*

Stephen H. Acunto was born on March 11, 1949, the son of Mercedes Bisordi and Stephen Berardini Acunto. He completed his education at New York University where he received his B.A. and M.A. degree in Classical Philology (Latin and Greek). Following graduation, Mr. Acunto taught classical literature, while publishing art, music and literary criticism in several leading periodicals.

Mr. Acunto is president of CINN, a vertically integrated group of companies in the insurance and legal publishing and communications fields. Among the company's publications the weekly *Insurance Advocate* founded in 1889, *La Follia,* the 110-year-old quarterly of Italian and Italian-American social and cultural affairs, and the *Italian Journal*, an academic quarterly on Italian social and economic topics, founded in 1948. His grandfather Michele Berardini was among the most successful Italian merchant bankers in the U.S. and Italy. Mr. Acunto remains active in Italian business and public affairs as U.S. Representative of the Bank of Saint Peter and Paul in Rome, as Chairman of the Italian Academy Foundation and publisher of its *Italian Journal.* In 1994, Mr. Acunto was appointed to the Board of Trustees of La Scuola New York. Later in 1997, he was appointed to the Board of Trustees of NYU's Casa Italiana. He chairs the Pro Italia committee that has sought Italy's entrance to the U.N. Security Council. He is on the board of the American Institute of Verdi Studies and is Chairman of the Westchester Opera Society. Mr. Acunto is the author of *Westchester County, a history and appreciation,* and is the Editor of *Giobbi: Representative Works.* He serves currently as an officer of the Insurance Federation of New York, The International Insurance Law Society, U.S. Chapter, and The American Reinsurance and Insurance Arbitration Society.

ROSA DE LAURO
United States Representative

United States Representative Rosa De Lauro was born and raised in New Haven's Wooster Square area. Her father, Ted, was an Alderman, and her mother Luisa, is the longest serving member of the New Haven Board of Aldermen.

A graduate of Marymount College, where she received her B.A. with honors, Congresswoman De Lauro received her M.A. in International Politics from Columbia University and studied at the London School of Economics.

She was first elected to Congress from Connecticut's Third District on November 6, 1990, and was reelected in 1992, 1994, and 1996. At the beginning of the 105th Congress, Congresswoman De Lauro was renamed to the Appropriations Committee, where she had served during the 103rd Congress. She sits on the Labor/HHS and Agriculture Subcommittees. During the 104th Congress she served on the National Security Committee. She was also honored with the appointment to the Democratic Leadership of the House and currently serves as Chief Deputy Whip.

Congresswoman De Lauro has been a strong supporter of health care reform, and she has introduced a bill to guarantee longer hospital stays for women undergoing mastectomies. In 1987, she served as an Executive Director of Countdown 87, the national campaign that successfully stopped U.S. military aid to the Nicaraguan Contras. From 1981 to 1987, she served as Chief of Staff to U.S. Senator Christopher Dodd.

1999 - Pepe's Pizza, Wooster Street, New Haven, Connecticut. The original "Pizzeria Napoletana" was established in 1925 by Mr. Frank Pepe. Mr. Pepe came to New Haven with his wife Filomena in 1911, from Minori, Italy. The business is still operated by his family.

1994 - Attorney Matt Naclerio at New Haven, Connecticut City Hall, during the swearing in ceremony for his first term as New Haven Alderman. His grandfather Matteo Naclerio, born in Italy, started the Foxon Park Beverage Co., which features the famous *Italian Gassosa*. The business is still operated by his family.

1994 - A traveling exhibit "La Storia Segreta," related the little known story of how at the outset of our involvement in World War II, hundreds of Italians in California, particularly in coastal towns, were labeled "enemy aliens," were forced to evacuate their homes and had to endure difficult travel restrictions and curfews. Ironically, many already had sons serving in the United States Armed Forces. Pictured at Southern Connecticut State University are, from left, Professor Eugene Fappiano, Professor Larry Pisani and Mia Di Stasi.

New Haven, Connecticut
1985 - Columbus Day Parade - The National Italian "Carabinieri Band."

GIUSEPPE MAZZOTTA
Professor of Italian Language and Literature - Writer

Professor Giuseppe Mazzotta was born in the region of Calabria, Italy in 1942. His father immigrated to Canada, and in 1957, Professor Mazzotta moved to Canada and lived in the Italian community in Toronto. In 1967 he transferred to the United States, first to Cornell University, where he received his Ph.D. in 1969. That same year, Professor Mazzotta joined the faculty of Romance Studies at Cornell University. In 1983 he moved to Yale University, where since 1996, he is the Charles C. and Dorathea S. Dilley Professor of Italian Language and Literature. Known widely as one of the most respected teachers at Yale, he is also an internationally known thinker of literary-historical and philosophical questions, such as the relation between literature, politics and theology. These questions he steadily probes in the several books he has authored over the years. In fact, he has dedicated his most recent book to the poetic philosophy of the 18th century Neapolitan thinker, Gianbattista Vico. Published by Princeton University Press in 1999, it is called *The Map of the World: The Poetic Philosophy of Gianbattista Vico*, and is being translated in several European languages. At the heart of Professor Mazzotta's intellectual vision stands the persuasion that a new model of thinking is needed and rapidly emerging in the western world. This new model, as one evinces from Professor Mazzotta's extensive writings, is the model represented and developed by the rich literary, artistic, philosophical and spiritual traditions of Italian culture. It is a culture shaped by the heritage of Rome, the Renaissance, and, more recently by the work of Gianbattista Vico. These are the ideas that inspire Professor Mazzotta's teaching and life. His other works in his field include books on Dante, Boccaccio and Petrarca. Among them *Dante's Vision and the Circle of Knowledge,* which was selected as one of the Outstanding Academic Books of 1993 by the *Journal Choice.*

1987 - Cardinal Anthony Bevilacqua, Archbishop of Philadelphia, at the Vatican with Pope John Paul II.

SISTER MARGHERITA MARCHIONE
President - Philip Mazzei Foundation

Sister Margherita Marchione was born in the town of Little Ferry, New Jersey in 1922, the daughter of Felicetta Schettino and Crescenzo Marchione, who emigrated from Italy in 1900. A Fulbright Scholar, she earned a B.A. at Georgian Court College in Lakewood, and continued her education at Columbia University where she received her M.A. and Ph.D. In 1941, she became a member of the Filippini Sisters Teaching Order. Sister Marchione is Professor Emeritus of Italian Language and Literature at Fairleigh Dickinson University, Madison, New Jersey. Sister Margherita is an internationally known author of over 30 books. They include literary figures Clemente Rebora, Giovanni Boine and Giuseppe Prezzolini and others. A member of the Religious Teachers Filippini, Sister Margherita is treasurer at Villa Walsh and president of the Philip Mazzei Foundation. As an international scholar, she will be best remembered for her work during the American Bicentennial Celebrations. With grants from the NHPRC, NEH, and other foundations, Sister Margherita dedicated ten years to researching and writing about Philip Mazzei's contributions to the creation of the United States. She also published Jefferson's *Zealous Whig* (1975) *My Life and Wanderings* (1980), and *The Adventurous Life of Philip Mazzei* (1985).

Besides lecturing in the U.S. and abroad, Sister Margherita has made numerous radio and television appearances. In 1992, she received The Philip Mazzei-Thomas Jefferson International Award in Florence, Italy, and the New Jersey Christopher Columbus Quincentennial Observance *Arts Award*. She is also the recipient of the Honorary Doctor of Humane Letters degree by Rambo College of New Jersey. She became an honorary citizen of both Poggio-a Caiano, Firenze, Philip Mazzei's birthplace, and Pontecagnano, Salerno, Italy, the birthplace of her parents.

FRANK J. DE SANTIS
National President - OSIA

Frank J. De Santis was born in Easton, Pennsylvania, the son of Margherita Luparelli and Giuseppe De Santis. He graduated from John Marshall High School in Los Angeles in 1950. After serving in the Korean war, he earned a bachelor's degree in Business from California State University, Los Angeles, where he later also earned a master's degree.

Mr. De Santis has successfully established several businesses and managed nonprofit organizations during his 40 year career. In 1997, he retired from Harbor-UCLA Research and Education Institute (REI), in Torrance, California, a nonprofit corporation affiliated with the Harbor-UCLA Medical Center. The institute currently administers 600 research and education grants and contracts covering a broad range of biomedical areas. De Santis directed the institute since 1962. During his tenure, annual expenditures for research grew from $55,000 to $50 million.

As national president of the Order of Sons of Italy (OSIA), Mr. De Santis directs the national and international activities of the oldest and largest national association of American men and women of Italian descent. He is also chairman of OSIA's two affiliated organizations, the Sons of Italy Foundation, a philanthropic institution, and the Commission for Social Justice, which fights discrimination and defamation against Italian Americans. Mr. De Santis also serves on the boards of the Medical Association Management Company (MAMCO), which he founded in 1972. MAMCO provides management services to several professional associations. He serves on the board of De Santis Enterprises, a family business that operates a group of pizza restaurants in Southern California. He has received many awards and honors, including the Italian Order of Merit Cavaliere, and Italy's Order of Merit Commendatore.

1989 - Cardinal Anthony Bevilacqua, Archbishop of Philadelphia, with John Paul II.

Washington, D.C. - The NIAF headquarters *(photo Paolo Galli).*
In 1998, the NIAF headquarters building was named "The Ambassador Peter Secchia Building,"
in honor of Ambassador Peter Secchia. The NIAF is the major advocate in Washington, D.C.
for over 20 million Italian-Americans.

JOSEPH V. SCELSA
Executive Director of The Calandra Italian American Institute - CUNY

Dr. Joseph V. Scelsa, a Bronx native, received his doctorate in Sociology and Education from Columbia University, and in addition, holds three Master's degree in Sociology, Social Studies and Counseling. He is also nationally certified as a Clinical Mental Health Counselor. In 1984, he was appointed Director of the Italian American Institute of New York, which was renamed the John D. Calandra Italian American Institute after the late State Senator John D. Calandra in 1987. In 1985, the Calandra Institute was afforded the status of a full university research institute through Queens College/City University of New York (CUNY) and Dr. Scelsa was elevated to Executive Director. Dr. Scelsa is Executive Producer and host of *ITALICS*: the Italian-American magazine which is co-produced by the Calandra Institute and CUNY-TV and seen on cable throughout the United States. He is considered an expert in Italian-American affairs, teaches and lectures extensively on Italian-American Studies and specializes in Italian-American and Civil Rights. He has authored and edited several books and has written various articles and reports on ethnicity, pluralism and education, notably the report on the *Italian-American High School Student Drop-out Rate in New York City Schools*. In 1992, Dr. Scelsa filed a federal civil rights lawsuit, Scelsa v. CUNY in the United States District Court, on behalf of the Calandra Institute and the Italian-American community against the City University of New York for anti-Italian discrimination. The landmark case marked the first time Italian-Americans were successful in bringing suit under United States Civil Rights statutes. Dr. Scelsa has received over 40 awards, among which is the rank of Ufficiale from the Order of Merit of Savoy for the work in the Italian-American community, and the Ellis Island Medal of Honor.

FRANK M. GRAZIOSO
President Connecticut OSIA

Frank M. Grazioso was born in New Haven, Connecticut, on March 26, 1939. He was educated in the public schools of the city and graduated with a Bachelor of Arts degree in 1961 from Yale College. In 1964, he attended the law school at the University of Chicago. After graduation, he began his law career in New Haven.

Throughout the years of his career, he has served in a number of public offices; as an alderman, as a corporation counsel, as a member of the Civil Service Commission, and as a member of the Board of the Harbor Commissioners.

He has participated as a leader in numerous charitable activities in New Haven; as Trustee of the Amity Charitable Trust, which awards scholarships to college bound students; as a trustee of St. Michael's Church, and as a member of the board of trustees of St. Raphael's Hospital Foundation. In 1992, Mr. Grazioso was appointed Treasurer and Counsel to the Bicentennial Commission. He also chaired the Columbus 500th anniversary celebration in Connecticut.

Mr. Grazioso was unanimously elected President of the State of Connecticut Order of Sons of Italy (OSIA) Grand Lodge with 18 local lodges in the State. In 1981, he was honored by the Italian government for his efforts on behalf of the Italian earthquake victims and was named Cavaliere in the "Order Al Merito della Repubblica." Mr. Grazioso has also received awards from the Connecticut Chapters of Sons of Italy, from the American Committee on Italian Migration and NIAF.

VITO M. MAZZA

President & Founder of Hunger Relief and Development, Inc.

Vito M. Mazza was born in New Haven, Connecticut, the son of Frances Battista Mazza and Vito Mazza. He was educated at Notre Dame High School in West Haven, where he was also an athlete. Later, he earned an Associate Degree in Business at Quinnipiac College and a B.S. degree in Business Administration at Columbia State University.

From 1956 to 1958, Mr. Mazza served in the United States Army as Cryptographer for the Central Intelligence Agency, receiving Top Secret Clearance. He served in Washington, D.C., Virginia and Asia Pacific, and received an honorable discharge.

Mr. Mazza entered politics for the first time in 1973, coordinating Mayor Johnson's campaign in West Haven, Connecticut. The following year, he ran for state office and was elected State Representative for the 115 District, serving for five terms, when Ella Grasso was Governor of Connecticut. In 1979, Mr. Mazza was invited to the White House by President Carter for briefing on National Affairs, and to meet Pope John Paul II on his historic visit.

Currently Mr. Mazza is a mayoral assistant in West Haven, and is the president of Hunger Relief and Development, Inc. a non profit organization he founded in 1984 dedicated to feeding, educating, and providing health care for the children of the Third World, principally Haiti.

Mr. Mazza is a member of the West Haven Italian American Civic Association. Since 1988, he has served as co-chair for the POW/MIA Memorial Service held at the State Capitol. He was also on the Board of Directors and Treasurer for the Connecticut Catholic Conference for five years.

THE MOST REV. PETER A. ROSAZZA
Bishop

Bishop Peter A. Rosazza was born in New Haven, Connecticut, on February 13, 1935, the eldest child of Agatha and Aldo Rosazza. He studied at St. Thomas Seminary in Bloomfield, Connecticut, and St. Bernard Seminary in Rochester, New York, later completing his four-years of concentration in Theology at the Seminare Saint-Sulpice in Paris, France. On June 29,1961, he was ordained a priest for the Archdiocese of Hartford in Notre Dame Cathedral in Paris.

Back in Connecticut he served as assistant pastor in the Church of St. Timothy in West Hartford and then was appointed to the faculty of St. Thomas Seminary where he taught French, Spanish and Italian.

In 1972, he became co-pastor of Sacred Heart Church in Hartford's north end, the mother church of Hartford's Hispanic Catholic community. In 1978, he was named Auxiliary Bishop by Pope Paul VI and was ordained Bishop on June 24 of the same year. Bishop Rosazza continued to minister at Sacred Heart until his transfer to Waterbury in 1981. In 1988 he was assigned to New Haven. On February 2, 1997, Archbishop Cronin appointed him Episcopal Vicar for the Hispanic Apostolate.

Bishop Rosazza is a member of the National Conference of Catholic Bishops' Committee on Migration and Refugee Services as well as Bishop Advisor to the National Catholic Student Coalition, and the National Catholic Young Adult Ministry Association.

VINCENT A. CIANCI, JR.
Mayor - Providence, Rhode Island

Mayor Vincent A. Cianci was born on April 30,1941, in Providence, Rhode Island, the son of Dr. and Mrs. Vincent A. Cianci. He was educated at Moses Brown School, and earned a bachelor's degree in Government at Fairfield University, a master's degree in Political Science at Villanova University, and a Doctorate of Jurisprudence at Marquette University School of Law. From 1966 to 1968, he served in the U. S. Army, where he received a Direct Commission as a Lieutenant in the Military Police Corps, and in the Army Reserves Civil Affairs Branch, through 1972. In 1967, he was admitted to the Bar, and later he was appointed Assistant Attorney General. In 1973, he became the prosecutor of the Rhode Island Attorney General Department's Anti-Corruption Strike Force. Elected Mayor for the first time at the age of 33 in 1974, Mayor Cianci, widely considered to be one of the most exciting and charismatic leaders in the City of Providence's history. Unopposed for re-election, Mayor Cianci took the oath of office in January 1999 for his sixth term, becoming the longest sitting Mayor in Providence's history. An outspoken champion of inner city revitalization, Mayor Cianci has received national recognition through his governmental career and, in 1996, was voted "America's most innovative Mayor" by the American Association of Government Officials. In the summer of 1997, Mayor Cianci was recognized by the *Utne Reader* and *Swing Magazine* as a champion of the arts.

Mayor Cianci has been awarded an honorary Doctor of Public Service degree by his almamater, Fairfield University. In July 1996, he was decorated by Italian President Oscar Luigi Scalfaro with the title of Grande Ufficiale.

DEAN MARTIN
Singer - Actor - Comedian

Dean Martin, the star of 51 motion pictures, was born Dino Crocetti on June 7, 1917, in Steubenville, Ohio, the son of a barber. He attended Steubenville High School, and at age 20 moved to Long Beach, California with his parents. Young Dino tried his hand at numerous jobs before taking up singing seriously. He was an amateur prize-fighter, worked in a service station, at a mill, and for a short time, as a croupier in a gambling house. Like most young men of the period who could carry a tune, Mr. Martin did impressions of Bing Crosby and other popular radio singers, and developed a pleasant, easy style all his own. By 1946, he was singing at the 500 Club in Atlantic City. On the same bill, at that time, was Jerry Lewis, whom Mr. Martin had met several times in the course of their young careers. When the club-owner found himself minus an act one night, Dean and Jerry induced him to let them go on as a double, and the team of Martin and Lewis was born. The audience loved them. The New York Copacabana opening was sensational, and drew attention from the East and West Coast. Later, producer Hal Wallis caught their act in a Los Angeles nightclub, and signed them to a motion picture contract, launching them on the screen in *My Friend Irma* in 1949. Eight years later, the team of Martin and Lewis was dissolved, and each went on to individual careers. His first solo starring role was in *10,000 Bedrooms*. Later, he switched from light comedy to heavy drama in *The Young Lions* and *Rio Bravo*. Other films followed, including *Some Came Running, Bandolero, Airport,* and *The Cannonball Run.* Mr. Martin also starred in his own television series for NBC-TV, and many of his recordings and albums have sold in the millions. He was the most successful man in show business, and in many respects the happiest. Mr. Martin died on December 25, 1995.

Anthony D'Alto standing by his home (rear) in Westport, Connecticut. He has opened over 100 Italian restaurants over his 30 year successful career. He provided work continuously for Italian immigrants, and helped many to start their own businesses. Mr. D'Alto and his wife Martha live in Westport. They have a son, Anthony D'Alto II, who is an attorney.

Ridgefield, Connecticut - One of Mr. D'Alto's Classic Italian restaurants "The Red Lion Belzoni Grill." The restaurant was named by Mr. D'Alto in honor of Giovanni Belzoni, an Italian explorer and archaeologist.

1985 - President Ronald Reagan speaks at the National Italian American
Foundation Annual Dinner, in Washington, D.C.

JOHN N. LA CORTE
Founder of the Italian Historical Society of America

John N. La Corte was born on July 4, 1910 in Jersey City, New Jersey. His parents emigrated to the United States from Sicily. When he was three years old, his parents returned to their homeland where Mr. La Corte remained until his 19th birthday. At that time, he had a choice of either remaining in Italy and forfeiting his American citizenship or coming to the United States to sign up for the American military draft. Mr. La Corte arrived on the shores of the United States with only 19 cents in his pocket, relying on the generosity of some cousins in New Jersey to help him establish his roots in this country. In New Jersey, he took up several different jobs to get by. Later he moved to Brooklyn, and started selling home appliances. His skills as a salesman paid off when he began to sell life insurance, becoming a high volume salesman. To the many families that he served, Mr. La Corte was more than a salesman taking care of insurance needs. He often helped them with immigration problems. One need of which Mr. La Corte was acutely aware was the severe defamation suffered by the Italians because of the well publicized criminal activities by a small group. He realized that the general public had forgotten about the great contributions that Italians had and were still making to the benefit of humanity. In 1949, he founded the Italian Historical Society of America. Mr. La Corte was instrumental and very successful in having the Verrazzano Bridge named after the true discoverer of New York, the Florentine Navigator, Giovanni da Verrazzano. Through his stewardship, the achievements of the society were truly monumental, particularly the acknowledgment of Antonio Meucci, of Joseph Bonaparte, the Founder of the Federal Bureau of Investigation, and Peter Caesar Alberti, the first Italian immigrant to this country among others.

ARTHUR BARBIERI
Democratic Town Chairman - New Haven, Connecticut

Arthur Barbieri was born in New Haven, Connecticut, on January 20, 1916, the son of Nancy D'Amato and Thomas Barbieri. He entered the world of politics at a very young age, helping out the Democratic party in his own ward on Clay Street in the Fair Haven section of New Haven, Connecticut.

In 1951, Mr. Barbieri was elected Town Clerk of the City of New Haven, winning the election with the Republican Mayor William Celentano. Two years later in 1953, he was elected New Haven's Democratic Town Chairman. Following his election to Town Chairman, Dick Lee, a Democrat, was elected mayor.

Under Mr. Barbieri's 40-year leadership, many Democratic candidates were elected, including Congressman Robert Giaimo and Joe Lieberman to Attorney General. There has not been a Republican mayor in office since. He became a good friend of Senator Tom Dodd, the father of Senator Chris Dodd, and was able to get money for the Redevelopment Agency of the City of New Haven, and other city projects.

Two young men, both students at Yale, Senator Joe Lieberman and President Bill Clinton, helped Mr. Barbieri in his headquarters to get the votes in for the Democratic candidates.

ANDREW N. FARNESE
President - Board of Education Philadelphia, PA - Deputy Attorney General

Andrew N. Farnese was born in Carini, (Palermo), Italy, the son of Vittoria Maiorano and Lorenzo Farnese. He was only 13 when he arrived to Philadelphia in 1927, where he attended public schools, graduating from Barratt Junior High School. Following his graduation from South Philadelphia High School, Mr. Farnese received his degree from Temple University (1937) and Temple Law School (1940) with a B.S. and Doctorate in Jurisprudence. He later established himself as an outstanding attorney and counselor. Although his legal skills were in great demand from major clients, Mr. Farnese always found time to serve the needs of the most humble client, including many Italian immigrants. His successful law practice soon attracted the attention of the corporate community which led to the founding of Lincoln National Bank with Richardson Dilworth, to the presidency of the Pfeiffer Foundation and General Compost Corp., and a directorship with Colonial Penn Life Insurance Company and the founding of William Penn Bank. He also served as an advisor to many international businesses. During World War II, Mr. Farnese served as an Army Ordinance Officer. Later, he served as Special Deputy Attorney General for the Commonwealth of Pennsylvania, followed by a term as Chairman of the Philadelphia Gas Works Commission. A former member of the Trial Court Nominating Commission of Pennsylvania, Mr. Farnese has also served as Vice President, and President of the Philadelphia Board of Education. During his term as President of the Board of Education, Mr. Farnese played a major role in the construction of the new Franklin Learning Center, providing additional classrooms for the Edmunds School, and the introduction of Little School Houses for pre-school classes. He has received numerous awards and honors.

JOHN ARCUDI
Chairman Compensation Commissioners

John Arcudi was born in Westport, Connecticut on May 26,1921, son of Mary Passafiume and Carmelo Arcudi. He attended Westport public schools and Yale University, where he received a B.A. in Economics and graduated from Yale Law School in 1947. He was an instructor in Economics at Yale College from 1946 to 1947.

Mr. Arcudi spent three years in the U.S. Army as an Intelligence Officer on General Patton's U.S. Army Staff. For that service, he was awarded the U.S. Legion Merit, and the French Croix de Guerre. He practiced law in Bridgeport until July 1, 1975.

In 1975, Mr. Arcudi was appointed Workers Compensation Commissioner by Governor Ella Grasso, with offices in the Greater New Haven area. In 1977, he became Chairman of the Board of Compensation Commissioners for the State of Connecticut. In 1981, he was appointed first full-time Chairman of the Commission in the State.

As Chairman of the Commission, Mr. Arcudi has been responsible for advice and consultation with the legislature on proposed worker's compensation legislation, the creation of the intra-agency appeals process in the Compensation Review Division, substituting that appeal for the appeal to the Superior Court.

Mr. Arcudi is a member of numerous professional civic, ethnic and religious organizations. In 1992, he was a member of the Connecticut Executive Committee, for the celebration of the Columbus 500th Anniversary.

1992 - In Philadelphia, PA, a three-sided memorial obelisk, 125 ft. high,
was erected to mark the 500th anniversary of Columbus's voyage.
The obelisk was donated by the America 500 Corporation, and is
located on Christopher Columbus Boulevard.

At age 100, Giuseppe Prezzolini, Professor Emeritus of Columbia University, with Sister
Margherita Marchione. This photo was taken several weeks before he died, on the terrace of
his apartment in Lugano, Switzerland, where he lived from 1968 until his death in 1982.

1985 - Sitting: Former Mayor of New Haven, Connecticut, Biagio Di Lieto and
Mrs. Rose Di Lieto. Standing: Father Salvatore Zocco with his sister Mrs. Maria Agnello.
Rev. Salvatore Zocco came from Italy in the early 1960's. He served in the
Archdiocese of Hartford, at St. Francis of Assisi Church, on Ferry Street in
New Haven, Connecticut, and is currently a Chaplain at St. Regis Health Center in New Haven.

The Southern Italy Religious Societies of New Haven, Connecticut.

New Haven - Connecticut
The Presidents of the Southern Italy Religious Societies.
From left: Anthony Vitolo, St. Maria Maddalena; Frank Gargano, St. Andrew;
Louis Longobardi, St. Catello; Anthony Rocco, St. Trofimena; Ruby Proto,
St. Maria delle Vergini and Teresa Argento, St. Andrew Ladies Society.

ROBERT G. TORRICELLI
U.S. Senator

Senator Robert G. Torricelli was born on August 26, 1951, the son of a school librarian and an attorney. He first showed his interest in public service by running for 5th grade class president in his Franklin Lakes, New Jersey elementary school. Although his father Salvatore, a second generation Sicilian immigrant, lost his bid to become mayor of Franklin Lakes, running on the same ticket, 14 year old Bob became the youngest person ever elected junior major.

Senator Torricelli went on to attend Rutgers College, where he was also elected class president his junior and senior year. In 1973, while still in college, Senator Torricelli worked on Brendan Byrne's successful campaign for Governor. After graduating, he enrolled in Rutgers School of Law where he earned his law degree, while also working as deputy Legislative Counsel to Governor Byrne. In 1980, he received his Master's degree in Public Administration from Harvard University's Kennedy School of Government. During the Carter administration, Senator Torricelli served in Washington as a counsel to Vice-President Walter Mondale, and while working at the White House, he went to Israel with the Vice-President to persuade then Prime Minister Begin to attend the Camp David peace talks. He proceeded to accompany Mondale to Egypt, to invite President Anwar Sadat as well.

In 1982, at the age of 31, the citizens of the 9th Congressional District elected him to the House of Representatives for the 98th Congress. He served for each successive Congress until 1996, when the people of New Jersey elected him to the United States Senate. In the House, Congressman Torricelli earned the respect of his colleagues and constituents. He is a member of the Government Affairs Committee, Judiciary Committee, Rules Committee, and Foreign Committee.

NANCY di BENEDETTO
Art Historian and Critic

Professor Nancy di Benedetto was born in Boston, the daughter of Ellen Gianferante and Vincent di Benedetto. She received a B.A. in Art History and English from Yale University in 1976, and a M.A. in Art History from Hunter College in New York in 1993. Currently, she is an Adjunct Professor at Marymount Manhattan College, where she teaches art and architectural history, collecting and connoisseurship, and literature.

Professor di Benedetto, in 1976, was named Assistant Dean at Pratt Institute's two year associate degree program. In 1978, she was named Administrative Dean of the New York School of Interior Design, and then Associate Dean of the State University of New York at Purchase. Her interests have always been in art and design education, art history and consulting, development and fundraising for non-profit organizations.

Professor di Benedetto has been President of the Yale Alumni Association of Metropolitan New York, and Co-Chair of the Alumni School Committee. She is a lecturer at the Metropolitan Museum of Art, Monclair Art Museum, and the English-Speaking Union. From 1984 to 1989, she served as the Executive Director of the New York Philomusica, Aston Magna Academy and Doing Art Together, managing areas of communication, marketing, board development and public relations.

Professor di Benedetto has written *History of American Art* for Bridgewater Press, and has written numerous articles and reviews for art magazines. During her career she has curated and juried many exhibitions nationally. She is a member of the American Associations of Museums, and a member of the American Branch of The National Trust of England.

New Haven, Connecticut - The Knights of Columbus, World Headquarters, a Catholic fraternal organization founded by Father Michael J. McGivney in 1882. When founded, the meetings were held in the basement of St. Mary's Church. To the right: The New Haven Coliseum.

 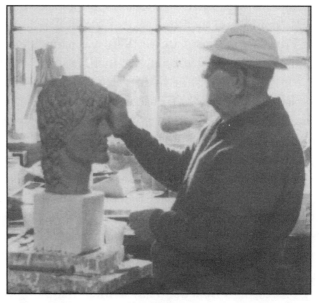

1979 - Peter Santos Saldibar was born in Udine, Italy, in 1907, and immigrated to America in 1912. He graduated from Yale School of Fine Arts in 1931. Mr. Saldibar was one of the most talented artists from Connecticut. His works include a plaque base relief sculpture of John Foster Dulles in Dallas Airport, various Vietnam War memorials and many others. On left: statue of Venus. Right: Mr. Saldibar working on the head of President John F. Kennedy.

RICHARD A. DAMIANI
Superior Court Judge

Judge Richard A. Damiani was born in New Haven, Connecticut, on January 25, 1946, the son of State Senator and City Court Judge B. Fred Damiani and Julia Adinolfi.

He attended parochial schools in the New Haven area and graduated from Providence College in 1967 with honors, where he was made a member of the Delta Epsilon Sigma honor society. In 1970, he graduated from the University of Connecticut School of Law with honors, and was admitted to the Connecticut Bar in 1970.

In September of 1970, Judge Damiani was appointed an assistant clerk of the Sixth Circuit Court and in January of 1971 he was appointed assistant prosecuting attorney of the Sixth Circuit Court.

Five years later, in 1976, he resigned his position as an assistant prosecuting attorney and entered private practice in the New Haven area.

After ten years of private practice, on November 6, 1985, he was appointed Superior Court Judge by Governor William O'Neil. Since his appointment as a Superior Court Judge, he has been the presiding criminal judge in various districts throughout the State of Connecticut.

Judge Damiani was married to Anna Marie Bonito on April 8, 1972, and has a daughter, Stephanie Ann.

ROSA TRILLO CLOUGH
Founder of the Center for Italian Studies - Florida

Dr. Rosa Trillo Clough, the daughter of Italian immigrants, was born and educated, for the most part in New York City. She studied at the Sorbonne in Paris and at the University of Florence in Italy. She received a B.A. degree from Hunter College, and an M.A. and a Ph.D. degree from Columbia University in New York City.

Dr. Clough was a Professor of Italian at Hunter College, later became chairman of the Modern Language Department at Finch College in New York City, and for three consecutive summers taught at the Middlebury Summer School at the College of Vermont and at Sarah Lawrence College in Florence, Italy.

She has written 10 books, three on Italian Futurism and several on Italian grammar and literature. Dr. Clough has also written many articles published in scholarly magazines such as *Italica, Books Abroad, The American Historical Review, L'Alighieri (Casa di Dante, Roma),* and in *Giornale d'Italia.*

Dr. Clough is the founder of the Center for Italian Studies in Palm Beach, Florida, and introduced the first Italian Adult Education courses at the Forest Hill High School several years ago. She has been teaching Italian in Palm Beach for many years and has recently written her 11th book, *Modern Italian Art.* She has been a member of many societies, and has received a number of awards. In 1995, Dr. Clough was elected to the "Hall of Fame" of Hunter College. In 1972, she was employed by Ambassador Claire Booth Luce to lecture on American Culture, in Italian, throughout Italy. She is also listed in the *Encyclopedia Britannica.*

ERNEST BORGNINE
Actor

Ernest Borgnine was born in Hamden, Connecticut on January 24, 1917. His parents had immigrated from Italy to Hamden. His mother took him back to Italy when he was two, but several years later they returned to Connecticut, this time to New Haven, where he completed his education through high school. From high school he went into the Navy, starting out at the bottom, he rose through the ranks to become, 10 years later, a Chief Gunner's mate. Mr. Borgnine knew he wanted to be an actor, and enrolled in the Randall School of Dramatic Arts in Hartford. From there, he broke into the professional ranks at the famous Barter Theatre in Virginia, where he painted scenery and drove a truck as well as acted.

Mr. Borgnine made his debut on Broadway as the hospital attendant in *Harvey*, and his career was officially underway. Since then, he has done dozens of films, and for television, over 200 live performances including such masterworks as *G.E. Theater* and *Philco Playhouse*. He played a brilliant part in the film *From Here To Eternity*, as the brutal stockade Sergeant, Fatso, and went on to become famous around the world for his Oscar-winning portrayal of the Bronx butcher, *Marty*.

His staggering number of outstanding film roles has made him something of an icon in the motion picture community. On his 80h birthday he was honored with an honorary Doctorate of Humane Letters from the legendary movie land film school, Columbia College-Hollywood. He has also been honored for his support of Navy Memorial Fund with the "Loner Sailor" Award from the Memorial Foundation. Mr. Borgnine lives in Beverly Hills with his wife Tova.

PETER F. SECCHIA
Former United States Ambassador to Italy

Peter F. Secchia was born on April 15,1937 in Englewood, New Jersey. He graduated with a degree in Economics from Michigan State University, and holds honorary doctorate degrees from several universities. Mr. Secchia is Chairman of the Board of Universal Forest Products Inc. (UFP), a Fortune 500 industrial company. UFP Inc. encompasses 51 manufacturing, wood preservation plants and distribution centers throughout the United States and Canada. He is also chairman of the River City Food Company, a company of 21 restaurants, catering and banquet facilities. Mr. Secchia served as the U.S. Ambassador to Italy from June 1989 through January of 1993. A vigorous proponent of personal voluntarism, Mr. Secchia has been involved in numerous political community and charitable concerns. In 1980 he was elected by his party to be Michigan's Republican Committeeman, and was also vice-chairman of the Republican National Committee heading its 13-state Midwest Region. He was host chairman of the 1985 RNC Midwest Leadership Conference in Grand Rapids. The conference was characterized by then Vice President George Bush as "the most successful regional conference ever held." He also received the Department of State Distinguished Honor Award for his success in U.S. foreign policy. His civic activities include past involvement and leadership roles in a wide spectrum of local and statewide charitable organizations. He is a member of the Grand Rapids Economic Club and the Grand Rapids Rotary. He is a director of the board of Old Kent Financial Corporation. Mr. Secchia is a member of National Italian American Foundation (NIAF), and the Washington D.C. NIAF headquarters is named "The Ambassador Peter F. Secchia Building." He was founding president of the West Michigan Lodge of the Sons of Italy in America. He is a close personal friend\advisor to former President Gerald R. Ford, and was a National Co-Chair of the Dole for President Campaign.

ELLA GRASSO
Governor - State of Connecticut

Governor Ella Tambussi Grasso was born in Windsor Locks, Connecticut May 19, 1919, daughter of Maria Oliva and Giacomo Tambussi. She attended St. Mary's School in Windsor Locks; Chaffee School in Windsor and Mt. Holyoke College, where she received a B.A. degree and in 1942, a M.A. degree.

In 1974, she was elected, as a Democrat, 83rd governor of Connecticut, becoming the first woman governor in the country on her own. She also served as a Secretary of the State from 1958 to 1969.

Governor Grasso was viewed by many as a liberal, but with her management skills, when it came to fiscal affairs, she demonstrated that she was very frugal and conservative on social policy questions such as abortion and welfare. Under her leadership, a major reorganization of state government was accomplished, merging more than 200 state agencies and departments. Her simple philosophy was "don't spend more than you receive, expenditure must not exceed revenue." She practiced what she preached, and her office was always open to people.

Governor Grasso resigned from office in December of 1980 due to illness. She died in Hartford on February 5, 1981, loosing the battle against cancer. Ella Grasso loved people, and was a good friend of the Italians of America.

1989 - Liberty State Park, New Jersey. Congressman Peter Rodino speaks
during the dinner in honor of the President of Italy Francesco Cossiga
at the Central Railroad Terminal, Liberty State Park.

Central Railroad Terminal, Liberty State Park, New Jersey, where more than eight million
immigrants set foot on U.S. land for the first time. The terminal was built in 1889.

Ministro Giorgio Radicati, Consul General of Italy in New York, was born in Rome on September 5, 1941. He received his law degree from the University of Rome. He began his foreign service career in 1967, and was nominated Vice Consul in Geneva in 1970. He was nominated Consul General of Italy in New York on November 1, 1998. Previously, in 1984, Ministro Radicati served as First Counsellor of the Italian Embassy in Washington, and in 1991, he was assigned to the Italian Embassy in Ankara.

1998 - Liberty State Park, New Jersey. "La Vela di Colombo" was unveiled on October 9, 1998, becoming the new Columbus Plaza on Liberty State Park, along the Hudson River, less than a quarter mile from historic Ellis Island. The sail has been donated by the Italian government. The NIAF, the Columbus Citizens Foundation and other private donors paid for the erection of the monument.

AILEEN RIOTTO SIREY
Founder of the National Organization for Italian American Women

Dr. Aileen Riotto Sirey was born in Brooklyn, New York. Her father was from Villa Rosa, Enna, and her mother's family from Graniti, Sicily. She is currently a psychotherapist in private practice in New York, and a faculty supervisor of doctoral students at the City University Clinical Psychology.

Dr. Sirey is the Chairwoman and Founder of the National Organization for Italian Women, and is Vice President for the National Italian American Foundation. Her energy and dedication to the Italian American community on behalf of women has had far reaching effects. Over the past 18 years, she has tirelessly dedicated herself to the development of a national and international network for women.

Under Dr. Sirey's leadership, the National Organization of Italian American Women grew to a membership in 27 states with regional programs in the Greater N.Y. Area, Western N.Y., Pennsylvania, Washington D.C. and Chicago. Through its many programs, the organization continues to serve the educational, professional, political and business aspirations of Italian-American women. Dr. Sirey has a special interest in the Mentor Program, which provides scholarships and guidance for graduate and undergraduate students as well as women returning to college later in life. She has written many articles related to the impact of culture and personality and she has developed a research project on Ethnotherapy for Italo-Americans. This project showed that self esteem is directly connected to understanding one's ethnic heritage and tradition. Dr. Sirey's professional achievements include teaching on the high school, college undergraduate and graduate level. In public health she was a hospital administrator and executive director of an agency providing training and technical assistance to providers of health services.

New York
1996 - Dr. Aileene Riotto Sirey with President Bill Clinton.

AL TERZI
Newscaster - WFSB Channel 3 - Hartford's CBS affiliate

Al Terzi was born on October 28,1942, in Little Falls, New York, the son of Alice and Armand Terzi. He earned a Bachelor of Arts degree in East Asian Languages (Chinese and Korean), following studies at Yale University and Central Connecticut State University. He also holds a law degree from the University of Connecticut School of Law in Hartford.

Mr. Terzi rejoined WFSB Channel 3, Hartford's CBS affiliate, in January 1994, having previously been employed by the station as a news anchor and talk show host.

In the interim, Mr. Terzi became even more well known to the Southern New England television audience while serving nearly 14 years as an anchor at WTNH Channel 8, the ABC affiliate in New Haven. He is considered by many the dean of the newscasters in Connecticut.

A military veteran, Mr. Terzi served more than seven years of active duty with the U.S. Air Force intelligence operations, working in the Far East, and later, as an instructor at a major air base in Texas.

During his career, Mr. Terzi has been the recipient of numerous awards, among them an Emmy Award for the New England region, The Boys Town of Italy Award, and has been Grand Marshal in the New Haven Columbus Day Parade. He lives in Connecticut with his wife and daughter.

ROSE MARIE BRAVO
Chief Executive - Burberrys Limited

In October, 1997 Rose Marie Bravo was named to the position of World-wide Chief Executive of Burberrys Limited, the British Luxury goods company.

Until her appointment at Burberrys, from 1992 she served as President of Saks Fifth Avenue, and was a member of the board of directors of Saks Holdings, Inc., where she was responsible for overseeing merchandising, marketing, advertising, and product development.

Ms. Bravo began her retailing career at Abraham & Straus (A&S) following her graduation from Fordham University in 1971. In 1974, she left A& S to join Macy's as an associate buyer. At Macy's, Ms. Bravo held a variety of positions in both the buying and merchandising of cosmetics, fragrances, accessories, fine jewelry, and ready-to-wear.

From 1987 to 1992, Ms. Bravo was Chairman and Chief Executive Officer of I. Magnin, the specialty division of R. H. Macy & Co., based in San Francisco.

Ms. Bravo has been honored for excellence in retailing by the National American Italian Foundation, The March of Dimes, City of Hope, Fashion Group International, and Marymount University. She sits on the board of the National Italian American Foundation and the advisory boards of both the Fashion Group International and The Fashion Institute of Technology in New York. Ms. Bravo is married and resides in Manhattan.

PAOLO VALESIO
Writer - Poet - Critic

Professor Paolo Valesio was born on October 14,1939 in Bologna, Italy, the son of Maria and Germano Valesio. He was educated at the Liceo Classico "Luigi Galvani," and completed his education at the University of Bologna graduating *summa cum laude.*

He came to the United States in 1963 to pursue his studies in language and literature. After spending three years at Harvard, Professor Valesio returned to Bologna to start a teaching career in Italy. In 1968 he decided to come back to America to be a lecturer and an associate Professor at Harvard. In 1973 he taught Italian at New York University. In 1975, Professor Valesio transferred to Yale University where he has been a Professor of Italian Language and Literature, and is currently the Chairman of the Italian Department. His interests have been in rhetoric, literature and spirituality, especially in the Renaissance and in the late nineteenth-century early twentieth-century period.

Professor Valesio is also a poet, a creative writer and a critic. He has published six collections of poetry, two novels and two volumes on short stories. Among his many publications, *L'ospedale di Manhattan* , and *S'incontrano gli amanti.* His dramatic poem in nine scenes, *Son of Man at Corcovado,* was performed in the town of San Miniato near Florence in the summer of 1993. At Yale, since 1993, he has been the organizer of "The Yale Poetry Group."

Professor Valesio has won two poetry prizes in Italy and one prize for literary criticism in the United States. He has been a Guggenheim Fellow, and he is the American correspondent of the Italian monthly magazine *Poesia.* He is also the associate director of the Italian Poetry Society of America.

Raffaele Sandolo with his wife Linda. Mr. Sandolo is the president of Oasis Coffee of Norwalk, Connecticut, one of the largest Coffee Roaster Companies in New England. He also owns several classic Italian restaurants in Southern Connecticut.

1997 - New York - Kerry Cuomo and Patrick Kennedy received the prestigious "3 I's" Award. The Award represents three countries, Ireland, Israel, and Italy. From left to right: Dr. Joseph Zagame, prominent philatelist; Professor Edward D. Re, Distinguished Professor of Law, St. John University; Kerry Kennedy Cuomo; the Honorable Patrick J. Kennedy, Congressman of Rhode Island; and Giuliana Ridolfi Cardillo, Istituto Italiano di Cultura.

PHILIP PAOLELLA
President Plasticrete Corporation

Philip Paolella was born in Hamden, Connecticut, on April 13, 1915, the son of Mary Jane and Ciro Paolella. He joined the family-owned Plasticrete Corporation in 1936 and became President in 1945, succeeding his father, Ciro Paolella, the founder of the firm.

In addition to his responsibilities of directing a major corporation, Mr. Paolella also served on the board of directors of the New Haven Savings Bank, Southern Connecticut Gas Company, and Southern New England Telephone Company.

Mr. Paolella, in 1970, founded the Italian American Historical Society, to promote and preserve the Italian heritage. In 1988, he was also the co-founder of the Ethnic Heritage Center, an organization of five ethnic historical societies, Italian, Jewish, Irish, Ukrainian and Afro-American. The five historical societies share archives and space for programming at Southern Connecticut State University in Hamden.

Over the years, Mr. Paolella has been recognized by many organizations for his humanitarian efforts and service. He received the Charles Carrol of Carolton Award from the Knights of Columbus and the Distinguished Service Award from the Jewish War Veterans of Hamden. He was also recognized by Rome with the presentation of the Papal Knighthood of St. Gregory, for his outstanding contributions to Catholic and civic organizations.

JOHN DE STEFANO, Jr.
Mayor - New Haven, Connecticut

Mayor John De Stefano, Jr., was born in New Haven, Connecticut, on May 11, 1955, son of Judy and John De Stefano. He attended the University of Connecticut, where he received a Bachelor's degree in Political Science and a Master's degree in Public Affairs.

After graduation from the University of Connecticut, Mayor De Stefano began to work for the City of New Haven as a Budget Analyst in the Controller's Office, serving later as the City's Deputy Controller, Chief Administrative Officer and Development Administrator.

In 1989, Mayor De Stefano left city government to become Executive Director of the Tennis Foundation of Connecticut, Inc., a nonprofit corporation that owns and operates the Connecticut Tennis Center, home of the Pilot Pen Tennis Tournament. In 1993, he decided to run for Mayor as a Democrat, and was elected New Haven's 49th Mayor. He was re-elected in 1995 for a second term, and in 1997 for a third term.

Mayor De Stefano is one of Connecticut's most visible and effective Mayors. The centerpiece of De Stefano's administration has been restoration of vital city services while decreasing the size of the city budget in his four years in office. He has been able to move city government closer to residents through the neighborhood-based delivery of services and by empowering citizens to get involved in shaping the life of the city.

MARIO B. MIGNONE

Executive Director of The Center For Italian Studies - SUNY

Dr. Mario B. Mignone was born in Benevento, Italy on July 26, 1940, the son of Palmina Iannace and Roberto Mignone. He came to the United States in 1960 with his parents, brothers and sisters. He received an M.A. in 1969, and in 1972, he earned his Ph. D. from Rutgers University.

Dr. Mignone began his teaching career in 1970 at State University of New York at Stony Brook, Long Island, when the Italian program only offered language courses. In 1988, he became Chairman of the Department of French and Italian at Stony Brook. The Department has now a faculty of seven full time professors, and offers a minor and major for undergraduate level, and for graduate level, M.A. and M.A.T., also a D.A. (Doctorate of Arts in Italian). Stony Brook is the only American University to offer a degree in Italian-American Studies.

Recognizing the importance of bringing back the huge Italian American community of Long Island to their cultural roots, in 1985, Dr. Mignone founded "The Center For Italian Studies." The Center promotes Italian culture, and organizes cultural activities in the Italian-American communities. In the past two years, the Center has received annual grants from New York State. In 1986, Dr. Mignone also founded the AIAE (Association of Italian American Educators) to promote the Italian culture in America. The AIAE gives out scholarships annually to dozens of Italian-American students. Dr. Mignone published many books, among which are *Italy Today: At the Crossroads of the New Millennium*, *The Theater of Eduardo De Filippo* and *Pirandello in America*. He is married to Lois Pontillo Mignone, and has three daughters.

MICHAEL VENA
Chairman Department Foreign Languages - SCSU

Dr. Michael Vena, son of Andrew Vena, was born on July 4, 1941 in Ielsi, Campobasso. He attended the Gymnasium and Liceo Classico "Mario Pagano" di Campobasso and completed his education in the United States where he received three degrees from Yale University in Romance Languages and Literatures, and his Ph.D. in 1972.

Dr. Vena was a lecturer at Yale from 1967 to 1974. In 1976, he was named Chairman of the Department of Foreign Languages and Comparative Literatures at Southern Connecticut State University, where he has been teaching. He has organized and directed for the past 20 consecutive years, a summer program at the University of Urbino, and an exchange program with Southern Connecticut State University.

Dr. Vena is well known in the field of Italian Renaissance, modern theater, and for language textbooks. He has published both here and abroad, is active at the local, national and international level and has served as president of a number of fraternal and professional organizations. He is a Fulbright Fellow at the University of Rome, a grant recipient from the National Endowment for Humanities, as well as from other State and Federal University programs. Dr. Vena was also an invited scholar in residence at the Italian Academy of Language in Florence.

Currently Dr. Vena is President of the American Italian Historical Society, of New Haven, Connecticut, and is still teaching at Southern Connecticut State University. He lives in Hamden, Connecticut, with his wife and children.

MARIA FOSCO
President of the Italian Welfare League, Inc.

Maria Fosco was born and raised in Astoria Queens, New York, the daughter of Filomena and Antonio Fosco. Her parents emigrated from Orsogna (Chieti), Abruzzo in the late 1950's. She attended Hunter College of the City University of New York, and in 1985 received a BA degree in History and Political Science. She earned a minor in Italian and studied Art History in Florence, Italy. Ms. Fosco has been employed by the John D. Calandra Italian American Institute of The City University of New York since 1986, and holds the position of Assistant Director of Resource and Community Programs. Ms. Fosco has been very active and involved in the Italian-American community for over 20 years. In 1992, when CUNY Chancellor W. Ann Reynolds dismantled the Calandra Institute, Ms. Fosco, in addition to giving important testimony during Temporary Restraining Order Hearing in Federal Court against the University on behalf of the Italian-American community, played a major role in preparing the case for trial (Scelsa v. CUNY) which eventually was settled. This case set precedent, for the first time Italian-Americans were recognized as a cognizable racial group. This case has become the most significant civil rights case in fighting discrimination against Italian-Americans in the United States. In 1998, Ms. Fosco was elected President of the Italian Welfare League, Inc., one of the oldest and most prestigious philanthropic Italian-American organizations in New York City, founded in 1920 by Mrs. Carolina Perera. In 1996, Ms. Fosco received the "Distinguished Service Award" presented by the Consul General of Italy Franco Mistretta on behalf of the Italian government in recognition of her outstanding contributions and dedicated service to the Italian community. She was also appointed to the board of directors of the Italian Heritage and Culture Month Committee.

GAETANO Di LEO
Publisher of *Italia E'* Magazine

Dr. Gaetano Di Leo was born in Milano, Italy on July 10,1947. He was educated at the University of Bari where he received a Ph.D. in Marine Biology. From 1978 to 1981 he was the director of the Acquarium of Valencia,Venezuela, the most important acquarium of North America.

In 1981, he came to America, settling in Miami where he earned a D.M.S. in fresh Water Ecology at the Florida Atlantic University. Dr. Di Leo was also on the faculty of the University of Miami to do research on the growth of shrimps. Three years later he received an M.B.A. in International Marketing & Finances from the University of Miami. In 1991, he started an international telecommunication company called "Mesunske Group."

Having been involved with the Italian community since he arrived to America, Dr. Di Leo decided to take over the bilingual magazine *Non solo pasta*, published in Italian and in English. As the new publisher, he changed the name of the magazine to *Italia E'*. It's purpose, to give important current information on the realities of today's Italy.

Dr. Di Leo has served as president of the Comites of Miami. He lives in Miami with his wife Gabryleda, who is the editor of the magazine, and she is also a researcher on Altzheimer's disease.

LAWRENCE F. PISANI

Chairman of the Department of Sociology and Anthropology - SCSU

Dr. Lawrence F. Pisani, the second of three children, was born in New Haven, Connecticut, on March 13, 1921. He was the son of Cavaliere Antonio and Dora Pisani. His father was a journalist for a New York Italian daily and publisher of his own weekly newspaper.

An honor student at Hillhouse High School, Dr. Pisani attended Yale University on a scholarship. His senior thesis was on the second Italian generation in America. He was awarded a fellowship by the Yale Graduate School where he earned his doctorate.

Dr. Pisani served on the faculty of the University of Massachusetts at Amherst and at the State University of New York at Binghamton, and at Southern Connecticut State University, where he was chairman of the Department of Sociology and Anthropology. He guided the department in developing a strong undergraduate and graduate program in sociology and anthropology. Upon his retirement in the fall of 1989, Dr. Pisani was designated Professor Emeritus of Sociology at Southern Connecticut State University.

An organizer and charter member of the American Italian Historical Society of New Haven, Dr. Pisani has served as President for several years. He is a member of NIAF and has served as panelist at several regional conferences. Dr. Pisani is also active with the Boy Scouts, Boys and Girls Club and the New Haven Gridiron Club. His awards and recognitions include the Silver Beaver (Boy Scout), St. George (Archdiocese of Hartford) and the Community Service Award (ACIM).

1992 - New Haven, Connecticut. On the occasion of the 500th anniversary of the discovery of America, U.S. Senator Joseph Lieberman and Alfonso Panico, president of the Columbus Day Committee, march in the New Haven parade in honor of Christopher Columbus.

October 10, 1992
Program

Welcome	Alfonso Panico, President
Invocation	Father Francis Minchiatti
Remarks by	Attorney Frank Grazioso
	Ralph Marcarelli
Wreath Laying	
Unveiling and blessing of stone	
Remarks by	Congresswoman Rosa DeLauro

1992 - The Columbus Day Committee Inc. of New Haven, Connecticut, on the occasion of the 500th celebration, unveils a stone at the statue of Columbus in New Haven. On left side are : Prof. Larry Pisani, Alfonso Panico, president Columbus Day Committee, and Dr. Ralph Marcarelli. On right side are: Stephen Papa, William J. Van Tassell, Knights of Columbus; Luisa De Lauro, Alderwoman, City of New Haven; Father Joe Moffo, and Congresswoman Rosa De Lauro.

EUGENE FAPPIANO

Former Chairman of the Department of Sociology and Anthropology
Southern Connecticut State University

Dr. Eugene Fappiano was born and raised in New Haven, Connecticut, (baptized at St. Donato Church). He is a graduate of Fairfield University (B.A.), and The New School for Social Research where he earned a Ph.D.

Prior to beginning his college teaching career, Dr. Fappiano worked briefly as an epidemiologist with the New Haven Health Department, where he was involved in some of this country's earliest research on lead poisoning.

He has been with the Department of Sociology and Anthropology at Southern Connecticut State University (SCSU) since 1967. During his tenure at SCSU, he has held the position of Department Chair, Graduate Program Coordinator, and Co-Chair of the interdisciplinary program in Criminal Justice Studies.

Dr. Fappiano is a member of the board of directors of the Italian American Historical Society of Greater New Haven, he is also co-editor of its newsletter *La Storia,* to which he regularly contributes articles.

Through the years, Dr. Fappiano has written articles on a variety of subjects in the *New Haven Register.* Among his varied interests and talents, he is also an accordion and piano player.

ANTHONY P. RESCIGNO

First Selectman - North Haven

Anthony P. Rescigno was born in New Haven, Connecticut, on February 26, 1945. He attended Wilbur Cross High School and later graduated from the University of New Haven with a B.S. degree in Business Administration. After spending 20 years in the business community, in 1989 he was elected First Selectman for the Town of North Haven.

Mr. Rescigno was employed by Plasticrete Block and Supply in a management position for 16 years, and then served as the Director of Parks and Recreation for the Town of North Haven for three years.

As First Selectman, Mr. Rescigno is a member of the Water Pollution Control Authority, the Board of Finance, the Cemetery Commission and is an ex-Officio member of all town Boards and Commissions. In addition, he is the former Chairman of the South Central Regional Council of Governments. He is also a member of the board of directors of the United Way of Greater New Haven and the board of directors of C.W. Costello, Company.

Most recently, he was appointed by Governor John Rowland to serve on the Department of Environmental Protection Task Force on Permitting and the State of Connecticut Resource Recovery Authority.

Mr. Rescigno has also served as the Republican Town Committee Chairman. On November 4, 1997, he was elected to serve a 5th term as First Selectman of the Town of North Haven.

RALPH MARCARELLI
Workers Compensation Commissioner

Dr. Ralph Marcarelli was born in New Haven, Connecticut on October 3, 1935. After graduating from Hillhouse High School, he received his A.B. from Fairfield University, and his M.A. in Italian Language and Literature from Middlebury College for studies completed at the University of Florence, Italy. He received his M. Phil. and Ph.D. in Italian at Yale University, where he specialized in Italian and Provencal Medieval and Renaissance Literature. While at Yale, he was the recipient of two University Fellowships, as well as the Sarah Page Hill Fellowship in Romance Languages and Literatures and the Lewis-Farmington Fellowship in the Humanities.

After completing his degree in Florence in 1961, he continued his studies at the University of Naples and was named Assistant Professor of English Literature at the Istituto Universitario Orientale. In 1963, he left Naples for Rome, where he worked as Coordinating Editor of *Unitas*, a quarterly review published in four languages and reflecting the thinking of the Holy See. Dr. Marcarelli returned to the United States in 1965 and resumed his teaching career, serving on the faculties of Albertus Magnus College, the University of New Haven, Southern Connecticut State University, the University of Rhode Island and Yale.

Long active in Republican Party affairs at all levels, he has been Chairman of the New Haven Republican Town Committee. He has been practicing Law in New Haven, and serves currently as Workers Compensation Commissioner, and Counsel to the Connecticut Republican Party. Dr. Marcarelli has been a leader in many charitable and civic organizations, and served also as a member of President Reagan's Neighborhood Policy Advisory Group.

New Haven, Connecticut
1981 - Dr. Ralph Marcarelli hosts President and Mrs. Nancy Reagan
while visiting Wooster Street in New Haven.

1998 - Fashion Designer Oleg Cassini with Josephine A. Maietta at a celebrity luncheon in his honor in Long Island, sponsored by the County of Nassau Office of Cultural Development.

1982 - New Orleans - Queen and Maids. Festa at Piazza D'Italia.

New Haven, Connecticut
May 13, 1994 - Dedication Ceremony of Mayor Biagio Di Lieto City Hall.

New Haven, Connecticut
May 13, 1994 - Dedication Ceremony of Mayor Biagio Di Lieto City Hall.
From left: Mayor Richard Lee, Mrs. Bartholomew Guida, Mayor Frank Logue,
Mayor Biagio Di Lieto, and Mayor John De Stefano, Jr.

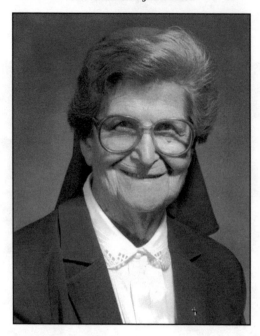

SISTER LOUISE ANTHONY
Chief Executive Officer of St. Raphael Hospital

Sister Louise Anthony Geronemo was born in Trenton, New Jersey, on January 16, 1914, the daughter of Louise and Anthony Geronemo. She came to New Haven, Connecticut, in 1935 when she entered the Hospital of Saint Raphael School of Nursing. After graduating, she received a Bachelor's degree from the Catholic University of America, later becoming supervisor of the Emergency Department and Outpatient Clinic.

Sister Louise Anthony was named hospital administrator in 1956 and served as chief executive officer until retiring in January 1979. Under her leadership, St. Raphael's became one of Connecticut's finest and largest community hospitals. During her tenure, Saint Raphael's opened the first radiation therapy treatment center in New England, and became the first community hospital in Connecticut to perform open-heart surgery and to open a coronary care unit.

As an administrator, Sister Louise Anthony served on many of Saint Raphael's boards, including those for the System, Hospital and Foundation. She was the first woman to serve on the board of directors of American National Bank, now Hudson American Bank & Trust Company. She was also the recipient of an honorary doctorate of Humane Letters from the University of New Haven and Albertus Magnus College.

In 1988, a new patient care building of the hospital named in her honor was dedicated. She died at age 83, on October 12, 1997.

1997 - The Italian American Historical Society of Greater New Haven.
From left: Professor Lawrence Pisani, President; Terry Gabucci;
Professor Eugene Fappiano; Mr. Philip Paolella, Founder; and Rose Mentone.
Missing from photo: Professor Michael Vena.

New Haven, Connecticut
Left: Sister Anne Virginie, President of the Healthcare System at St. Raphael Hospital.
Right: Dr. William F. Verdi (1872-1957) Founder of St. Raphael Hospital.
He was Chief of Surgery at St. Raphael's from 1907-1953.

JOEL SCHIAVONE
President - Schiavone Corporation

It's hard to describe New Haven, Connecticut, in the 1960's and early 1970's. The extent of the urban decline and devastation was enormous and widespread. For a period of 10-15 years, virtually every landmark in the City was closed, including the Taft Hotel, the Shubert Theater and the Palace Theatre.

Task force after task force came up with ideas and concepts as to how to solve the problem with no progress. Frustrated about the continued decline, and the inability of any other agency or corporation to make an impact, Joel Schiavone formed the Schiavone Realty and Development Corporation and began to purchase buildings downtown. By 1984, all these buildings were restored and, for the most part, leased. With all this leasing activity, Yale gradually opened its doors and people mysteriously appeared on the streets, almost around the clock. In particular, the area took on a reputation as the entertainment center of the region. Restaurants proliferated, a substantial number of nightclubs opened and, most importantly two theaters — The Shubert and The Palace — reopened. The Palace was owned and operated by the Schiavone Realty and Development Corporation. The Shubert Theater was reopened by a joint venture of the Fusco Corporation and Schiavone Realty and Development Corporation. The theaters, in conjunction with the other activities in the area, brought thousands of people into downtown New Haven for the first time in years. Fifteen years later, the district is still the heart and soul of the city. Other activities are taking place now, in the 1990's, and hopefully, the entire mosaic of the nine squares will once again be vibrant.

Mr. Joel Schiavone was the City Republican Town Chairman, he ran for Governor in 1989, and was the Republican-nominated candidate for State Comptroller in 1990.

JOHN P. AMBROGIO
Chief of Police

John P. Ambrogio, was born March 25, 1934 in New Haven, Connecticut, son of Rose Del Grego Ambrogio and William Perri Sant Ambrogio. He attended local schools, and in 1952, after graduation from high school, he served in the U.S. Army at Fort Belvoir, on the administrative support staff of the engineering school from 1953 to 1955.

On September 5, 1974, Mr. Ambrogio was appointed Chief of Police for the town of Hamden. Prior to his appointment, he held the positions of Detective Sergeant, Training Officer and Deputy Chief.

Chief Ambrogio is the recipient of the 1997 Milton S. Camilleri Award for his unwavering support of the efforts of Connecticut police officers fighting the war against drugs and for a career dedicated to the professional advancement of police service.

He is a past president of the Connecticut Chiefs of Police Association, and sitting member of Police Officers Training and Standard Council. Chief Ambrogio served on the Legislative Committee and Firearms Committee of the body. He has been instrumental in drafting significant legislation dealing with criminal law and cooperation among various police agencies.

Chief Ambrogio is married to Maureen O'Connor and has five children: four daughters and one son.

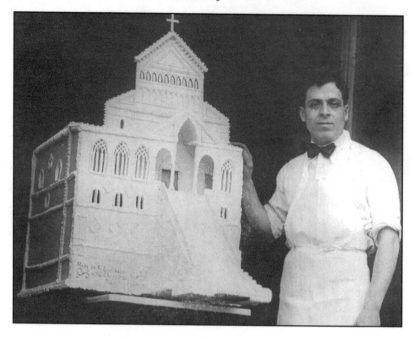

FRANCESCO LUCIBELLO
Original Owner of Lucibello's Pastry Shop

Francesco (Frank) Lucibello was born on August 23, 1897 in Amalfi, a small village on the Costiera Amalfitana of Southern Italy, the son of Salvatore and Marialfonsa Lucibello. He served in the infantry of the Italian Army during World War I. After his discharge from the army, he emigrated to the United States, arriving in New York City in 1920. Mr. Lucibello remained in the New York area while he learned and became an expert pastry baker. In 1929 he married Filomena Proto, who was also an immigrant from Atrani, a town near Amalfi. Later the couple moved to New Haven, Connecticut, where Mr. Lucibello opened an Italian pastry shop.

During the depression, Mr. Lucibello decided to utilize his occasional free time to create a replica in sugar of the world famous Cathedral of Saint Andrew in Amalfi. This creation demonstrated the artistic ability of the young baker and remained on display in the bakery window for many years. The cathedral replica provided many of the area's residents with a nostalgic reminder of Amalfi.

Mr. Lucibello's talent was not limited to pastry baking and sugar sculpture. His teaching priority to numerous apprentices, beside teaching skills, was about a very high standard of work ethic. He trained two young workers that went on to open their own pastry businesses. One of them was Frank Faggio who took over his business upon his retirement in 1958. Lucibello's pastry shop became an institution in New Haven. Today the pastry shop is located on Grand Avenue and Olive Street, and run by Frank Faggio's son Peter. Mr. Lucibello was a strong advocate of education, often expressing his regrets for not having been able to go on with his own. However, he continually urged his young workers to pursue advanced education. His daughters, Norma and Mary are both college graduates.

1989 - Frank Faggio and his wife Anne, owners of the Lucibello's pastry shop in
New Haven, Connecticut. Lucibello's Italian pastry shop was established in 1929 by its
original owner, Mr. Frank Lucibello. Mr. Faggio took over the business in 1962, relocating to
Olive Street and Grand Avenue. Mr. Faggio died in 1992. The pastry shop is now
operated by Mr. Faggio's son Peter Faggio.

Phil's Barber Shop, serving the Yale community, was established in 1929. Phil's has two loca-
tions, on Broadway and Wall Street, in the heart of Yale University in New Haven.

JOHN LA BARCA
Radio Show Host

John La Barca was born on September 14,1947 in Brooklyn, New York, the son of Maria and Anthony La Barca. He has been a popular morning show host at numerous metropolitan area radio stations since he was eighteen, and is currently heard in the morning on WICC - 600 AM. Mr. La Barca is also an actor, appearing on film in *Godfather Part I.* He has performed in many theatrical endeavors such as children's theater at the famous Westport Country Playhouse in Westport, CT, as a funny dancing Winnie The Pooh. The youngest of four boys in a struggling, hard-working environment, Mr. La Barca learned very quickly to respect his roots. He always participated with great pleasure in family gatherings, particularly on special holiday food fests where his father would take out the accordion and everyone would sing Italian songs. Through his career, Mr. La Barca has dedicated his life to helping great humanitarian causes, raising hundreds of thousands of dollars for numerous organizations; the Sons of Italy, cancer research and veteran groups. He is a multi-decorated Vietnam veteran, and has received dozens of awards for his humanitarian efforts.

Mr. La Barca hosts the number one-rated Italian-American radio program in the country at WICC - 600 AM in Bridgeport, Connecticut. For five hours, every Sunday from 9 a.m. to 2 p.m., he entertains with wonderful old and new Italian and Italian-American songs, along with his 88-year-old mom as a co-host making the dialogue extremely funny, and passionately nostalgic. Mr. La Barca, through his radio programs, has hosted many concerts and has even appeared many times on television to promote Italian-American causes.

BARBARA A. DENICOLA
Mayor - Hamden, Connecticut

Mayor Barbara DeNicola, a lifetime resident of Hamden, Connecticut, was the daughter of Anna and John De Nicola. She attended the Hamden Public School System, graduating from Hamden High School in 1950. She received her Bachelor's Degree in History and earned a Master's degree in Guidance and Administration from the University of Connecticut. She also obtained her six year certification in educational administration from Southern Connecticut State University.

Mayor DeNicola has had the privilege of working in numerous Connecticut School Systems, in a variety of teaching and administrative capacities. In 1990, she retired as an Associate Superintendent in the Hamden School System.

Earlier in her career, Mayor DeNicola had the opportunity to spend several years as an educator and administrator overseas in Turkey, France and Japan. In November 1997, she was elected Mayor of Hamden. Previously, Mayor DeNicola's father, John Sr., served as First Selectman and was the Town's first Mayor. Her brother John Jr. also served as Mayor.

In 1998, Mayor DeNicola received the Community Service Award from the American Committee on Italian Migration.

CIRO GUASTELLA
Chairman of the Board - One Call Users Council, Inc. - N.Y.

Ciro Guastella was born on July 4, 1941, in Marineo, Italy, the son of Gaetana and Giuseppe Guastella. His father died when he was two years old. In 1966, he came to America to join his mother and his older sister in Astoria Queens.

In 1973, Mr. Guastella married his wife Joyce and went to work for AT&T in the building department. He has remained at AT&T for the past 25 years, and has moved on, becoming the AT&T damage prevention representative in the New York City and Long Island area, representing the company in the One Call Center program, and helping millions of people by doing his job.

Mr. Guastella has served as president, and is today the chairman of the board of the One Call Users Council, a non-profit organization that oversees the One Call operation and concerns itself with safety practices to reduce on-the-job-injuries. The organization also oversees that underground damage prevention is accomplished by minimizing expenses and delays, with the objective to deliver uninterrupted vital services such as electric, water, gas and communication linkages so necessary to the modern urban survival. Most utility company operators (Con Edison, Bell Atlantic, Empire City Subway, AT&T, Brooklyn Union Gas, Buckeye Pipeline, Lilco, Time Warner etc.) that own underground service lines are participating members of the One Call Program.

Mr. Guastella is very active in political and social organizations, he lives in New York with his wife, and his children Gordon and Marisa.

ANTHONY V. AVALLONE
State Senator

Anthony V. Avallone was born in New Haven, Connecticut on December 6, 1947, son of Anthony S. and Virginia Avallone. He attended Morris Cove and Nathan Hale Schools in New Haven, and Notre Dame High School in West Haven. After earning his Bachelor of Arts degree from the University of Connecticut, Mr. Avallone went on to earn a law degree from Suffolk University in Boston, Massachusetts.

In 1982, he was elected to the State Senate, becoming one of the few first-term legislators ever honored with the appointment to chair a standing legislative committee. Mr. Avallone was reelected for four additional terms, serving also as the Chairman of the Judiciary Committee, one of the most powerful and influential committees in the General Assembly. He was also the Chairman of the Commerce and Exportation Committee.

In 1984, Mr. Avallone was the chief sponsor of passed legislation that made Connecticut the first state in the nation to have statewide emergency 911 telephone service, to ensure that citizens throughout the state will receive the fastest possible response to calls for help.

He is an attorney in New Haven, and is an active member of innumerable community, civic, and religious organizations. Mr. Avallone is married to Patty Bishop, and has two sons, Brian Anthony and Jonathan Douglas.

— A TRIBUTE —
MARCELLO MASTROIANNI

A man loved by all

Marcello Mastroianni was born on September 28, 1924 in Fontana Liri, near Frosinone, Italy. In 1950, he married Flora Carabella, and they had a daughter Barbara. During his career he made over 150 films, and was considered one of the greatest actors. He loved his work, he loved people, and he loved life. Among his many films, Fellini's *La Dolce Vita; Divorce Italian Style; Yesterday, Today and Tomorrow; Marriage Italian Style; A Special Day; City of Women; Ginger and Fred* and *Three Lives and Only One Death,* in which he played four parts. In the same film was his actress daughter Chiara Mastroianni, born to Catherine Deneuve in 1972. Mr. Mastroianni died in Paris, December 19, 1996, at the age of 72.